For the Good of the *Women*

Thomas M. Daly

For the Good of the Women

Library of Congress Catalog Control Number: 2004093371
ISBN: 0-9755241-0-0

Design and layout by Kyla Dimond & Erin Harrison

Daly Publishing
2311 W. 105th Street
Bloomington, Minnesota 55431

Dedication

To Jackie Fleming who told her staff,
"Remember, you're here for the good of the women."

Acknowledgements

Special thanks to Pam Toepper, Delores Host, and Barb Hanson for their assistance at MCF-Shakopee, to Shari Burt at the Department of Corrections Central Office, to Judith Hentges at the Scott County Historical Society Museum, to the library staff at the Minnesota Historical Society, to Eileen Welsh who read early versions of the text and gave encouragement, to Tom Melchior who edited out most of the errors, and to my wife Pat who gave kind support while losing the use of the dining room table for long periods of time.

Photo courtesy of the Minnesota Historical Society

Isabel Davis Higbee 1849-1915

It was Thursday, March 4, 1915. The weather was typical for early March: cold with predictions of snow. Isabel Higbee knew that her heart was failing, but she was determined not to fail the women for whom she had been fighting for more than twenty years. Since the mid-1880s, women leaders in Minnesota had been asking lawmakers for more decent treatment of women who were convicted of crimes. Isabel Higbee had been asked to testify against a bill being considered at the legislature. The bill would have continued housing women at Stillwater Prison, separate from the men, but in a more jail-like setting. Punishment, not rehabilitation, was the order of the day, but the winds of change were blowing.

Isabel told her friends that her heart was bothering her. She said, "...I am going to continue to fight, even if I die in the harness." Just before she went to attend the committee hearing at the capitol, she gave her friend a sealed letter and said, "Put it in your handbag and if anything happens, open it."

She and about 50 other women who opposed the bill under consideration went to the capitol that evening. Women could testify at legislative hearings, but they could not vote in elections or hold public office. In fact, earlier that same day, the state senate had defeated a bill to give Minnesota women the right to vote.

Isabel Higbee stood and faced the men across the committee room, across a gulf that custom, law and privilege had created. Women should not be housed at Stillwater Prison she told them. Women need a special place, a reformatory, a place that would provide a humane and healthy environment that would help them return to society as contributing members. "Freedom," Isabel said, "is the test of a penal institution.... We must give the women fresh air, God's glorious sunshine, and as much freedom as is consistent with discipline." She was having some difficulty speaking. With great effort, she spoke her last words to the committee, "...I shall trust to your judgment to accord us a women's reformatory."

Isabel Higbee took her seat and the next woman began to speak. Then Isabel started coughing, fell back in her chair and lost consciousness. Friends rushed to her side. A doctor was called for and arrived quickly, but too late. Isabel Higbee had died. It was 9:15 p.m. at the capitol and snow began to fall.

By morning more than six inches of snow covered the Twin Cities with a white shroud, and news of Isabel Higbee's death was on the front page of the Minneapolis and St. Paul newspapers. Articles concerning her life, death, funeral, and her will continued to appear in the newspapers for the next two weeks.

The envelope that she had given to her friend, Mrs. J. C. Joyslin, contained a note with helpful information that many of her friends might not have known: " Isabel Davis Higbee, born in Warren, Vermont, April 24, 1849. Parents: Joshua and Eleanor Davis. Came to Minnesota in 1870. Minneapolis was her first home. Married Dr. Higbee Jan. 17, 1876, and came to St. Paul. Commenced teaching school in Vermont at age of 14 and continued teaching school in Vermont and Minneapolis."

The St. Paul *Pioneer Press* carried the death of Isabel Higbee as its most prominent front-page story. A second article quoted several women leaders who suggested that a women's reformatory would be a fitting memorial to her and that a building there should be named after Mrs. Higbee. Mrs. L. A. Hamlin was quoted as saying, "St. Paul owes more to Mrs. Higbee than to any other woman...She was a force for every good movement which has been carried to success in Minnesota." Mrs. Albert Hall said, "Mrs. Higbee gave her life for the girls of Minnesota. The state, in her death, loses the most valuable woman we have. She has done more for our girls and women than any other individual or organization in the state."

The Minneapolis *Journal's* front-page story included the resolution passed earlier in the day by the Minnesota House of Representatives: "Whereas Death entered this chamber last evening and removed from this life Mrs. C. G. Higbee while working for the benefit of her sex and the uplifting of humanity. Resolved that this house express its high appreciation of her services to the people of this state and its deep sorrow at her sudden and untimely death."

On Sunday, March 7, 1915, the St. Paul *Pioneer Press* reported, "For the first time in Minnesota legislative history the women's organizations are united to push one project above all others. It is the women's reformatory." The paper estimated that about 150,000 women were represented by the Minnesota Federation of Women's Clubs, the Federation of Fraternal Women, W.C.T.U. and the Minnesota Suffrage Association. The article went on to say that three separate bills related to the subject were scheduled for consideration by the House the following Wednesday. A more detailed picture of the extraordinary Isabel Davis Higbee evolved in the newspapers during the next few days.

Isabel Davis was born in Warren, Vermont in 1849. Apparently she was both bright and precocious; she began her teaching career in Vermont at the age of fourteen. Isabel moved to Minneapolis in 1870 and taught at Washington School where she was known as Miss Belle Davis. She became the principal of Jackson School in Minneapolis prior to her marriage to Dr. Chester G. Higbee in January 1876.

Following their marriage in Minneapolis, Isabel and Dr. Higbee lived most of their life together in St. Paul where he had begun practicing medicine in 1874. The Higbees built a house at the corner of Ninth and Robert Streets. Dr. Higbee, a Civil War veteran 14 years older than Isabel, became one of St. Paul's leading physicians. Their home was known for the care and hospitality that the Higbees extended to family, friends and strangers. They adopted a daughter Lorna, and were foster parents for several nieces and nephews.

Like many intelligent, educated, socially concerned, and caring women, Isabel Higbee became more and more involved in learning about societal problems and doing something about them. She and thousands of women in Minnesota and across America joined the women's club movement. In St. Paul the Fourth District Women's Club provided her with opportunities to learn and to lead. Eventually her leadership abilities took her beyond St. Paul, and she became the state president of the Minnesota Federation of Women's Clubs from 1907 to 1911.

Isabel spoke out on issues that ranged from conservation and civic responsibility to homelessness and prison reform. Most often she spoke out for the needs of women and children, the poor, and the downtrodden. She learned that there is power in numbers. At a meeting of women in Sauk Centre, she said, "There was a time when individual effort was sufficient to meet social needs, but life has grown so complex that organization is absolutely necessary."

Over the years Isabel Higbee led the way on many issues. She helped to establish the Bethel Boat, a houseboat homeless shelter on the Mississippi

River in St. Paul. The Bethel Boat evolved into the Bethel Hotel and today it is run by the Union Gospel Mission. Isabel also began the Bethel Mothers' Club and the practice of friendly visiting of poor families. In addition she was one of the founders of the St. Paul Newsboys Club, which was set up to help the ragamuffin boys who sold newspapers on the city streets.

Isabel helped to create the State Arts Commission and the women's department of the State Labor Bureau. She was instrumental in getting women hired as policewomen in the City of St. Paul. For the latter effort, the St. Paul Chief of Police presented her with a gold star.

Two of her most satisfying achievements were helping to get the state legislature to establish the Minnesota Home School for Girls at Sauk Centre in 1907 and selecting its first superintendent, Fannie French Morse, who became nationally recognized as an expert on issues dealing with the treatment of girls and women. Not surprisingly, Mrs. Morse and Mrs. Higbee became good friends.

Getting the legislature to provide a suitable facility for girls was easier than getting a similar place for women. Isabel Higbee and the other women who shared the vision to provide humane treatment for women had been asking lawmakers to grant their request for more than 20 years. Once the Home School for Girls was a reality, the women hoped to take the next step.

When Isabel Higbee died at the legislature, the next step came quickly. The reaction was immediate. One woman said, "...no man can refuse us the reformatory when it is realized that women are willing to give up their lives for it." The legislature responded rapidly. Funds were allocated. A search for an appropriate site was undertaken. One hundred and sixty-seven acres on the edge of the town of Shakopee were purchased. Like the Home School for Girls, the women's facility would be based on the cottage system. It would include a farm and there would be no bars or wall or perimeter fence. Its main building was named Isabel Higbee Hall and a bronze plaque on its wall would explain:

Isabel Higbee Hall
This building so named in grateful appreciation of the life and labors of Mrs. Isabel Higbee who died March 4,1915, in the state capitol at St. Paul after pleading for the establishment of this institution.

Proponents of the cottage system envisioned relatively small living units and humane, nearly family-like, living conditions. At Shakopee there would be plenty of fresh air, sunshine, and the opportunity for women to work on the farm that was the greater part of the rural estate. When completed in 1919, Isabel Higbee Hall was a handsome, two story, brick building. Its second floor contained eighteen individual rooms for the women, a large general assembly room, a dining room, bathrooms, and matron's rooms. There were no locks on the doors or bars on the windows, but an annunciator system was used. In the evening whenever an inmate's door opened, a light flashed and a bell rang in the matron's room. Reform and rehabilitation, not punishment, were intended to be the rule here.

On the first floor were a hospital wing, operating and treatment rooms, offices, staff rooms, one large kitchen, and the superintendent's living quarters. The first superintendent said that the loveliest part of her quarters was the porch from which she could see "the twisting valley, with flashes of the Minnesota River and the dipping background of hills."

The basement of Higbee Hall included a laundry room and a large room that became a sewing room in the early years. In later years it became the education area with a classroom and the institution's library

Additional cottages were built in the next six years: Anna Howard Shaw Cottage in 1920, Maria Sanford Cottage in 1922, and Susan B. Anthony Cottage in 1925. Each of the newer cottages had rooms for 21 women. With the completion of Anthony Cottage in 1925, the institution's capacity was 81 women. Anthony Cottage was built into the side of a hill which allowed it to have full-length windows on one side of its basement. The sewing department that included 20 sewing machines by 1925 was moved into this basement and made good use of the natural light.

With the completion of Isabel Higbee Hall in 1919 and the necessary laws to allow the transfer of women from the State Prison in Stillwater, one very important task still needed to be done: finding the right person to become the superintendent of this new reformatory for women. The Board of Control began to look for a person with "a modern outlook, a solid training, a deep interest in women and children, and ... health and enthusiasm." They found that person in Florence Monahan.

Florence Monahan was born in Chicago in 1890 and moved to Minneapolis with her family about 1900. She attended St. Cloud Teachers College and earned a degree in 1908. Florence taught in several towns including Moorhead and Minneapolis. While teaching at Corcoran School in Minneapolis, she continued her own education by attending law school at night. She finished the four-year course in three years. In fact, she was the valedictorian of the class of 1917 at Northwestern College of Law. Florence Monahan passed the Minnesota State Bar in June 1917.

In addition to teaching mathematics by day and English three nights a week to Russian immigrants, Florence studied the law and found time to become very active in the women's suffrage movement. As a member of the Minnesota Women's Suffrage Association, she became a speaker and organizer in Minnesota, South Dakota, New Jersey and New York. These activities brought her into contact with many of Minnesota's leading men and women. One of them was Mrs. Clara Ueland, who not only became a friend and mentor but also opened the door that led Florence Monahan to Shakopee.

In 1917 Florence was becoming eager to use her new law degree. She spoke to her friend Mrs. Ueland, who in turn wrote a very complimentary letter praising Florence to Mr. Charles E. Vasaly, the chairman of the Board of Control. The Board of Control was responsible for overseeing the operation of the new reformatory for women. At that moment in 1917, Mr. Vasaly had no job opening for this bright, energetic, well educated, young woman, but in two years he would.

Late in September 1919, Florence Monahan was working for the Children's Bureau. She had taken a position as a caseworker and was attempting to protect the lives of mothers and children under new laws that had recently taken effect. She looked up from her desk to see the secretary of the Board of Control, Mr. Mullen, standing in her office. He said that the members of the board wanted to see her. The boardroom was just across the hallway.

Florence Monahan described what happened next. "It was a much disturbed young woman who entered the board room. The three members, Mr. Vasaly, Mr. Charles Swendseen, and Mr. Ralph Wheelock, sat in a handsome and imposing row. Mr. Vasaly, a courteous and kindly gentleman, at once put me at ease by asking me to sit down. Fortunately, I sat; I was totally unprepared for his next statement. Even watching his lips form the words, I could not believe what he was saying: 'We want you to be Superintendent of the new Reformatory for Women at Shakopee.'"

Florence tried to argue that she lacked knowledge and experience, but they argued that she had what they wanted and they would help with any problems. She asked to see the reformatory before giving a final answer. The next day was Sunday and she toured the empty new reformatory and its grounds thinking of the challenges and possibilities. On Monday she said, "Yes."

The board members instructed Florence to visit every reformatory for women in the United States and to learn what to do and what to avoid. There were sixteen modern reformatories for women; Florence began immediately to learn about penology first hand.

A high point of her tour was meeting Mrs. Jessie Hodder, the superintendent of the State Reformatory for Women at Framington, Massachusetts; the low point was visiting Sing Sing Prison's death house. About Sing Sing Florence wrote later, "No more drab, desolate scene could be imagined, and beyond the partitions – unseen but screaming, yelling, cursing, sounding more like wild animals than human beings – were twenty-six doomed men. The memory has never left me."

At Bedford Hills Reformatory for Women in New York, Florence witnessed a young woman being subdued and handcuffed with her arms in a "torturous position." She promised herself "no matter what happened I would never lay hands on any girl or woman in my charge." But there were positive lessons to be learned at Bedford Hills also. Florence noticed that one of the matrons who fed her charges best was also the most economical in the use of supplies. The matron's name was Mrs. Curran. When Florence Monahan learned that Mrs. Curran had resigned her position, she immediately contacted her and hired her at Shakopee where Mrs. Curran performed admirably and provided valuable advice.

Back home in Minnesota, Florence Monahan went shopping with $7,000 given by the Board of Control to furnish the reformatory. For the assembly room, she purchased rocking chairs, books and a piano; for the dining room, she selected round tables for four and matching chairs that the women could paint. For the women's rooms, Florence decided on cot-beds and dressers plus curtain material that the women could dye or decorate. Regarding her purchases, she wrote later, " I wanted the illusion of a home; I wanted the atmosphere at Shakopee as far removed as possible from the gray stone I had seen at Sing Sing."

On December 29, 1919, Florence Monahan moved into her quarters in Isabel Higbee Hall; 34 hectic days later, the first inmates arrived at the reformatory. The 15 women inmates at Stillwater were sent in small groups. This allowed the matrons at Stillwater to be laid off gradually, and it allowed Superintendent Monahan to gradually build the culture of the new reformatory. "Send us women who can work," she requested.

Monahan felt she needed a cook, a seamstress, a waitress, and a scrubwoman. When the first four women arrived, she gave them a number and a job. Number one went to Marie; she had murdered her husband; she would be the cook. Number two went to Old Rose; she was addicted to dope and drink; she would be the seamstress. Number three went to Addie; she was a combination prostitute, shoplifter, and drug addict; she would be the scrubwoman/housekeeper. Number four went to Frances; she was in for shoplifting and prostitution; she would be the waitress.

That same afternoon, Shakopee's first commitment arrived from court. June became number five; she was a forger and a drug addict; she would be a general helper. So that was the beginning on February 2, 1920.

About 20 years later in her book *Women in Crime*, Florence Monahan wrote the following:

"This motley assortment – murderess, prostitute, shoplifter, drug addict, forger – formed the nucleus of our new reformatory, and, although the population increased, the type of clientele stayed the same. A survey of Shakopee during my superintendency showed that of the first 78 inmates, average age twenty-seven, the crimes for which they were committed ran as follows: bigamy, 6; taking life, 7; forms of stealing including forgery, 47; miscellaneous, including sex delinquency, 18."

Monahan held a personal interview with each new inmate. "The therapeutic value of talking things out in the beginning cannot be overestimated," she wrote. The women might lie or tell the truth, but the interview was the beginning of their journey together. The goal was rehabilitation.

After the initial interview the women received physical examinations including their eyes and teeth, good food, decent clothes and surroundings, work to do, and kind and sympathetic treatment. But this was not enough to bring about any genuine change in character. The women must desire to change. "How to stimulate this desire," Monahan declared, "is the real problem in any reformatory program."

Some of the women who arrived at Shakopee had little or no experience with normal housework and manners from taking a bath to using forks, knives and spoons at the dinner table. Two of the women who transferred from Stillwater Prison cried when they first saw their "real rooms" with beds, dressers and chairs.

At Shakopee the women were expected to work eight hours a day, six days a week. They were taught all phases of housework. Some were assigned to work across the street at the reformatory farmstead where a farmer and his male assistant did the heaviest work, but the women took care of chickens and pigs, milked the cows, shocked grain, weeded asparagus, and picked vegetables and fruits including strawberries and gooseberries.

The sewing room was the other major work area. In her first biennial report to the Board of Control for the period ending June 30, 1922, Florence Monahan wrote:

"We aim to teach plain sewing to every woman. To do this we maintain a sewing room, where we not only do all the sewing for the institution – making dresses, coats, underwear and everything used – but we also sew for other institutions. We have made during the past fifteen months: 906 dresses, ranging from four-year old to eighteen-year old sizes. No two dresses are made alike; the women learn to design and cut them. We have made 134 winter coats, 972 boys' waists, 240 pairs of bloomers, 564 nightgowns, 48 work shirts and 12 babys' bonnets for the State Public School at Owatonna. For the hospitals for the insane, we have made 780 shirts, 560 nightshirts, 600 union suits, and 180 nightgowns."

In her 1922 report Monahan also said that the women were decorating their own rooms and other rooms in the institution using simple and inexpensive materials to make curtains and painting unpainted furniture. Women were also given responsible jobs in the office, storeroom, laundry, and on the farm. They were paid for their work from six to fifteen cents per day, and once a month they were allowed to shop through the superintendent's office for items such as toilet articles, fancy work, or candy.

"At Stillwater," Monahan wrote, "the women had worn ugly gray chambray uniforms of separate skirts, full-gored and long, and shirtwaists with tight, wrist-length sleeves and high-to-the-chin collars. For warmth they wore old fashioned shawls and looked like immigrants." At Shakopee there were no uniforms.

The women made their own dresses of various plaid ginghams. They wore colored dresses on weekdays and white ones on Sundays. When working on the farm or on the grounds, mowing lawns or gardening, the women wore work clothes including straw hats and khaki trousers. The clothing was affected slightly by the grade system which was used to determine a woman's status in the institution. There were three grades: one, two and three. Women were placed at grade two when they arrived and would remain there for five months. If they showed good behavior, they would be promoted to first grade. Misbehavior would result in marks against them and an accumulation of marks would cause them to be demoted to third grade. Grades were indicated by the wearing of collars: third grade wore no collars, second grade wore collars to match the dress, and on first grade white collars were worn. Thus good behavior was rewarded and inappropriate behavior resulted in loss of privileges rather than direct punishment.

"Shakopee," wrote Florence Monahan, "was never a center of sentimentality, nor was it a place of vengeance." Women did not wear uniforms, march in lock step on straight lines painted down the hallways, nor were they beaten with steel tipped canes for minor infractions like the men at Stillwater. There were no guns, guard towers, or prison walls at Shakopee; nevertheless, as she observed, "...one thing makes the place a prison: all inmates must rise, dress, eat, sleep, study, work, play, retire at another's will."

Certainly the relatively low number of inmates and the cottage system helped Florence Monahan and her staff provide humane treatment for the women at Shakopee, but a great deal of credit goes to Monahan herself. Alice Ames Winter in an article in the *Ladies Home Journal* described Monahan in 1925, "So Shakopee begins with Florence Monahan, big, handsome, wholesome, buoyant with that kind of buoyancy that seems irresistible." At five feet nine inches Florence described herself as more of a truck than a racehorse, but surely it was her heart and mind, her intelligence and intuition as well as her energy and physique that carried the day and allowed Shakopee to move along the path of reform rather than punishment.

Good food, hard work and fresh air were three of the ingredients that Florence thought were absolutely necessary, and there was one more: recreation. She wrote, "I believe that after a full day's work people need play and exercise and I encouraged recreational activities. In summer the entire play period (6:00 – 8:30 p.m.) was spent out-of-doors and the women enjoyed baseball, croquet, pitching horseshoes. In winter they sat around the fireplaces in the homelike cottage living-rooms, furnished with rocking chairs, a piano, books, and good pictures, and read, sang, played games, and prepared programs for their own amusement."

Long walks on Sundays began in the spring of 1920 and were eventually abandoned, not because of any attempts to escape, but because the prison population had grown too large and resembled a parade. Sleigh-rides were also introduced followed by hot chocolate, sandwiches and warm baths, "a good night's rest and a zest for the morrow's work."

During her first summer at Shakopee, Florence Monahan began a tradition that particularly pleased her, the Old Settlers' Picnic. She declared that inmates who had served "two or more years consecutively" would be allowed to accompany her on a daylong picnic at the nearby Minnesota River. The picnickers for that first picnic were the fifteen inmates who had transferred from Stillwater in February. "A lunch of all the things they liked – bacon and eggs, sandwiches, salads, cakes, fruit and candy – was packed in wicker hampers," she wrote. "Carrying them, we walked a mile or so off the grounds to a tree-shaded spot at the river's edge where we built a fire, cooked our meal and ate it under the spreading elms."

The women spent the afternoon wading in the river or walking in the woods; one woman went off by herself, but returned after several hours as Monahan thought she would. A woman who was serving a life sentence told the superintendent, "I never believed I'd ever again feel as free as I have today." After singing songs and having late afternoon tea, they all walked back up to the reformatory at sunset, the superintendent and her 15 "old-timers."

Not every inmate was able to resist the temptation to run away from this prison without bars, walls, or fences. In the first two and a half years, five women escaped. Although four were returned to Shakopee, it was decided that the temptation to run was greatest for the newest inmates. As a result bars were placed on the windows of eight inmate rooms in each cottage, and all newly admitted women were placed in these rooms. This solution apparently was a wise one; there was not another escape for six years. Shakopee continued to have no perimeter fence or wall for the next 80 years, yet all women who were convicted for committing felonies in Minnesota were sent there.

In 1921 the state legislature passed the Habitual Offenders Act that provided that anyone convicted three times within five years of a misdemeanor involving moral turpitude might be declared to be a habitual offender and be sent to prison. By June 1922, four women were committed to Shakopee under this law. Many reformers and other well-intentioned people had promoted the passage of this law. They felt that it was better for a woman to be sent to a reformatory for an extended period of time than to be constantly in and out of jail with no apparent change in her public behavior.

By July 1,1924, the inmate population had risen to 63; the average age had risen also to nearly 31 years old. Reflecting on these facts, Florence Monahan wrote, "This increase does not to us indicate more women are becoming criminals but rather is the result of the action of the Habitual Offender Act; and also the change in attitude of the courts which causes them to deal as severely with women offenders as with men offenders."

After more than four years as superintendent, Monahan was convinced that the approach she and her staff were taking with the women was appropriate. She wrote the following in her report to the Board of Control:

"Our policy of disciplining more by loss of privileges than by direct punishment has continued and proved successful. The paying of a small wage, from six to fifteen cents a day is a great help in maintaining order and establishing a good spirit. We have never had any serious trouble with discipline, and generally have very little difficulty of this kind. This I attribute largely to two material reasons and one emotional one. The material reasons are that the women all work eight hours a day and that they are fed plenty of well-cooked wholesome food. Added to this is the feeling that our attitude toward them is friendly and helpful. They know we are trying our best to help them to be better citizens."

Another indication that Florence Monahan believed in the program that she and her staff were creating is the fact that in May 1925, she offered Shakopee as the site for a ten state regional conference for the Committee on the Care and Training of Delinquent Women and Girls. Approximately 70 participants listened to lectures, held discussions, ate meals, and shared entertainments for three days. Twenty of the participants lived in Isabel Higbee Hall during the conference. The inmates who had been living there moved out temporarily to the newly completed Susan B. Anthony Cottage.

The conference was a success. Monahan later observed, "We could not have managed if the inmates had not cooperated to the hilt...It is well known in institutions that at unusual times the inmates arise to the occasion remarkably well." The inmates did everything from registering the guests, to waiting on tables and entertaining. Commenting on the inmates' participation, Florence Monahan said, "They were just as much interested in making the conference a success as we were."

Two of the participants at the conference were Mrs. William E. Lewis and Mrs. Charlotte Butler of Chicago. They were very impressed with what they saw at Shakopee and with Superintendent Florence Monahan. They wondered if it would be possible to lure her away to Illinois. In seven years, they would have their answer. Meanwhile, Shakopee's reputation continued to spread throughout America and beyond. Visitors came from Australia, China, Holland and Sweden. Shakopee's reputation was becoming worldwide.

By July 1, 1926, the inmate population rose to 80. Every room was occupied except one. Superintendent Monahan requested an additional cottage and expansion of the heating plant at the institution. She was denied the improvements. Two years later the inmate population reached 96 and the women in Higbee Hall were double bunked. Disciplinary problems increased with the overcrowding. The main work area, the sewing room, employed 60 women, but the women were forced to work in silence because of their numbers. Life was becoming more difficult for the inmates and the staff. Once again, the superintendent requested that an additional cottage be built. The board denied her request.

In that same biennial report, Florence Monahan reflected upon a central truth in all rehabilitation programs: "Unless a woman herself wishes to change, no improvement can be made in her character. We aim to first have a woman see herself as she really is, to realize what brought her to this state in life, and then to encourage her to so change herself that she can go out and earn her living as a decent woman."

Relief came in August 1928 as the inmate population began to decline. From June 1929 to June 1930, the inmate population hovered between 60 and 70 women, well below the capacity of 81. Florence Monahan tried to analyze the decline in population and came to the conclusion that the courts were extending greater leniency to women who were being arrested. Perhaps the Depression was also having an effect.

In her report to the State Board of Control for the period ending June 30, 1930, Superintendent Monahan wrote: "We have never feared to ask for suggestions from inmates. Almost every year we allow them to ask for privileges or changes which they think would make life here pleasanter. We do not agree to make these changes but are glad to listen to the suggestions. They have usually been surprisingly easy to grant with no increase in disciplinary trouble. Do not think this is coddling; for no institution which segregates a group, takes away liberty of action, demands constant obedience, requires living away from family life, can be anything but an abnormal, hard life. Whatever we can do, while maintaining the necessary discipline and order, to alleviate these severe conditions ought to be considered."

Monahan also surveyed all of the inmates who were discharged either from parole or directly from Shakopee during the previous year by sending them a written survey that asked them to respond to questions about life in the institution and changes that they might suggest. About one-third of the inmates responded even though they were entirely beyond Shakopee's control. Florence hoped to incorporate their suggestions into future improvements at Shakopee particularly in the area of leisure time activities.

On January 1, 1930, Miss Evelyn C. Gran resigned from her position as Shakopee's parole agent. She had served since the very beginning in 1920 and had been very important in helping women make the transition back to society. Florence Monahan wrote, "We were very sorry to lose her loyal, devoted, unfailing services..."

During the next six months Florence Monahan and Miss Susan Rogers shared the duties of parole agent and Monahan wrote the agent's biennial report for the period ending June 30, 1930. The superintendent took the opportunity to reflect upon the previous ten years of parole work. She wrote, "Looking back over our last ten years of parole work we find that 140 women have been on parole. Of these, 104 were successful and discharged; 36 were unsuccessful and returned to this institution." Monahan went on to note that of those who had been successful, 18 percent had previous delinquency records; of the 36 unsuccessful ones, 50 percent had previous delinquency records. She pointed out that the parole system for women depended upon finding suitable places for the women to live and work, and it was equally important to find good women to supervise the parolees. Upon the latter point Monahan wrote, "On the whole we have been very fortunate in finding a group of educated, intelligent housewives who year after year take our girls on parole." The fact that 74 per cent of the women who were paroled were successful in making the transition back to society is a tribute to Florence Monahan, her staff, Evelyn Gran, those intelligent housewives, and the women inmates from Shakopee.

The inmate population continued to decline, and in May 1931, it was agreed that Shakopee take federal women prisoners at $1.25 per day. As of June 30, 1932, there were 53 state prisoners and 12 federal prisoners at Shakopee. Disciplinary problems declined with the declining population. Educational programming which had always existed to some extent, particularly for illiterate women, was now extended to all inmates for at least one hour per day.

In 1931, Florence Monahan went to the annual congress of the American Prison Association (now the American Correctional Association). Mrs. William E. Lewis, who had visited Shakopee in 1925 and had stayed in contact with Florence over the years, sat down with her in a hallway at the conference and said, "We want you to come to Geneva, the Training School for Girls."

Although Florence's initial reaction was, "Oh, no; not that place," she visited Geneva on her way back to Minnesota. She found it "very old fashioned and musty, filled with unhappy, regimented girls and old women matrons," but her friends from Illinois were persistent in wanting her to take the position of superintendent at Geneva. In the next few months she gauged the challenge of applying her theories to a younger group of women against staying at Shakopee where she had tenure and was not subject to politics. In Illinois the leaders of the women's clubs wanted a woman like Florence Monahan, who could create a system of rehabilitation for girls emphasizing education, recreation, and exercise rather than fear and isolation as currently existed. On February 1, 1932, nearly 12 years exactly since she had welcomed her first inmates at Shakopee, Florence made a phone call to Illinois. "I'll come," she said.

"And with those words," she wrote later, " I ended a rich and colorful chapter in my life. For twelve years my chief interest in life, asleep or awake, day or night, wherever I was, was Shakopee; I had given it everything I had in the way of thought, energy, executive ability. It was my child in a sense that no other institution could ever be."

In her last biennial report to the State Board of Control, Florence Monahan wrote: "In concluding twelve years of work in this institution, I am filled with gratitude for the cooperation and support received from your Board, from a loyal hard-working staff, and from a large proportion of the women sent here as prisoners. This helpfulness on the part of all concerned with the institution has made it possible for us to accomplish whatever has been done."

In the years that followed Florence Monahan's departure, the institution benefited from a series of able superintendents. Each contributed elements to the institution which confirmed that it was not so much bricks and mortar as it was flesh and blood, hopes, aspirations, and ideas. At its core was a vision for better lives for the women in its care.

Ruth T. Devney, the first superintendent to follow in Monahan's footsteps, assumed her duties on April 15, 1932. She wrote an addendum to the biennial report submitted by Florence Monahan in which she expressed her gratefulness for the "clean, well-equipped and well-regulated institution."

During her two years as superintendent, Ruth Devney focused on several areas: psychological services, library services, education, and recreation. Devney expanded the use of IQ testing and the services of psychologists from the State Research Bureau, which, she hoped, would help in understanding the women better and in grouping them educationally. She improved the library services for the women by creating a centralized library in the Main Building, organized and directed by Miss Perrie Jones, State Librarian. Devney was also interested in the role education played in the rehabilitative process. In addition, she mentioned that only a few women seemed to cause most of the disciplinary problems in the institution, and she felt that there was a constant need for the services and advice of a psychiatrist. Finally, she hoped to provide a more organized recreation program for the women.

Extreme weather conditions increased during the 1930s. Drought reduced crop production on the reformatory's farm, but the farm was still able to provide an ample supply of root vegetables for the institution plus all the milk, butter, eggs, poultry and pork used by the women. The weather was less of a factor for the sewing industry. Sewing continued to provide the garments that the women needed and clothing for the other state institutions.

On May 1, 1934, Estelle Jamieson became the third superintendent. Like her predecessor, she wrote an addendum to the biennial report: "My impression is that the institution is but a Boarding School where all are learning the 'Art of Living.'" Two years later Jamieson requested that one section of Higbee Hall be equipped for maximum security and segregation. Apparently not all of the "boarders" were learning the "Art of Living."

Devney and Jamieson shared an interest in IQ testing of the inmates. The 1934 biennial report included for the first time a section entitled "Psychological Report." It reported that 20 of the 60 inmates were "morons" and that 38 of the 60 inmates were "below average IQ." Although some people might question the validity of such testing, it may help to explain the increased use of the term girls by both superintendents in their official reports.

The biennial report in 1934 contained more narrative sections including one by an inmate librarian who reported that the library had been moved to a "small but pleasant room" on the main floor of Higbee Hall. The library contained about 800 volumes, 14 magazine subscriptions, encyclopedia and reference books. The school report by instructor Dorothy Grandquist indicated that the school day ran from 8 a.m. to 10 a.m. and from 1 p.m. to 5 p.m. with physical education on Mondays, Wednesdays and Thursdays from 7 p.m. to 8 pm. The women were receiving instruction in subjects ranging from basic skills to shorthand, typing and more advanced topics.

The report also included a section entitled "Girls' Rules" which listed 30 rules that the women were expected to obey. Although not particularly harsh, the rules seemed unnecessarily controlling and petty. For instance, rule #14 was "No talking on walks in passing between buildings." Isabel Higbee's vision of a reformatory with "as much freedom as is consistent with discipline" was fading somewhat with the passing years.

In the biennial report for 1935-1936, Superintendent Jamieson wrote that a Catholic priest and a Lutheran minister were holding a non-sectarian worship service on alternate Sundays. Inmate attendance at these devotions was mandatory.

On a lighter note, the superintendent also reported that the women held a style show at which they modeled clothes that they had designed and sewn. On the recreational side, the inmates organized two kitten ball teams, and they played young women's teams from the towns of Shakopee and Chaska.

President Roosevelt's New Deal programs, intended to combat the Great Depression and get America back on its feet, were good for Shakopee. Jamieson reported that the women enjoyed concerts at the institution provided by the F.E.R.A. (Federal Emergency Relief Administration) orchestra and the

P.W.A. (Public Works Administration) orchestra. In addition, federal funds and workers were used to build a five-car garage in the basement of Shaw Cottage and also a brooder house on the farm.

State funds, however, were not so easy to obtain, and the buildings were beginning to show their wear. Superintendent Jamieson pointed out in her report that after 15 years all four buildings needed roofing, painting and masonry repairs plus repairs to floors and equipment. The farm cottage and barn, which were much older than the rest of the institution, needed to be replaced. These requests went largely unanswered. The inmate population continued to hover between 70 and 80 during the middle 1930s; normal wear and tear on the buildings continued.

In 1935 several factors combined to launch a new era in Shakopee's history. A new teacher, Mary Anne Toner, was hired who had the talent to teach journalism. The inmate population of 75 contained enough talented women to staff an inmate newspaper. A new mimeograph machine was purchased, and Superintendent Estelle Jamieson gave her blessing. The *Reflector* was born in November 1935 with its first issue. It was a well written and lively monthly newspaper (ten issues per year) filled with articles about various aspects of the institution and also original inmate poems and editorials. One of the inmate editorials made its way into the *Congressional Record* when it was incorporated into a speech by Representative Alexander.

In September 1938, the inmate staff outdid themselves with a 27 page special edition of the *Reflector* that was used to welcome members of the Prison Congress who were meeting in St. Paul. It began with a short history of the 18-year-old reformatory, starting with Isabel Higbee and concluding with the words "great improvements have been made in the institution under the able and kindly administration of Superintendent Estelle Jamieson whose advanced ideas in penology have placed Shakopee in the front rank of women's prisons." The history neglected to mention Florence Monahan whose 12 years of work shaped the first two-thirds of the institution's existence. Monahan noted the oversight in her book by pointing out that after leaving Shakopee in 1932, "Six years later I read a history of the institution in which my name was not even mentioned."

Never the less, the special edition was quite remarkable. It contained past articles and editorials, poems, cottage reports, sports articles, and went into detail describing various programs. It highlighted the music program, which featured Walter Damrosch's radio broadcasts each Friday night; it boasted that the library had grown to 1600 volumes. It pointed out that the education program included religious and ethical classes, vocational classes in shorthand and typing (though not at present), and the sewing department was "a school as well as an industry." The paper praised the recreational program for activities that ranged from kitten ball to dancing and included not only performances by local musicians, but also off-grounds activities. Three times in the previous year inmates attended movies at the local movie theater. Finally, Miss Mary Anne Toner, teacher, education director, and editor-in-chief of the *Reflector*, received well-deserved praise.

In 1939 the State Board of Control passed into history and was replaced by the Department of Social Security, Division of Public Institutions. To them Estelle Jamieson addressed Shakopee's *Tenth Biennial Report, 1939-1940*. The institution's population averaged 75 in 1939 and 76 in 1940. The average age of the inmates was 33, and the median IQ was reported as 67.85. The superintendent reported that the 160-acre farm was utilized in the following ways: 131 acres – cultivated, 20 acres – pasture, and 9 acres – lawn. Also the farmhouse, which was nearly 100 years old, was repaired in 1939. The institution's staff was comprised of 18 persons, 12 women and 6 men.

Federal funds continued to provide special programs. In January 1940, the WPA provided an art instructor from the Walker Art Center, who offered the women instruction in pencil, charcoal, and watercolor. Music and drama classes were also offered, and the teacher was funded by the Federal Adult Education Program. The women were also encouraged to create their own programs in their cottages, and they responded with music, dancing, and their own amateur plays. The sewing program was still strong. The superintendent reported that the women produced 12,316 pieces of clothing during the biennium. There were few discipline problems during this period. Inmates were allowed to smoke two cigarettes per day.

The inmate population peaked in 1940 with an average daily population of 76 and then began to decline. In April 1941, Shaw Cottage was closed. The average daily population for fiscal 1941 was 60 inmates. In the fall of 1941 when a new federal prison for women was opened in Texas, most of the federal inmates at Shakopee were transferred.The United States went to war on December 7, 1941. As Americans turned their attention to the war effort, Shakopee's population continued to decline. In March 1942, Anthony Cottage was closed; all of the women were now housed in the two remaining buildings, Sanford Cottage and Isabel Higbee Hall. The average daily population for the year ending June 30, 1942, was 43 inmates.

The war years saw prison populations decline around the country. Staffing the reformatory became more difficult as the demand grew for workers in factories and men and women in the armed forces.

Patriotism flourished at the reformatory. On Flag Day 1942, a new flag and flagpole were dedicated. The women contributed to the war effort by sewing and knitting garments for the Red Cross and by purchasing savings stamps with their meager earnings. Nineteen women took the Red Cross Standard Course in First Aid, and on August 3, 1943, women inmates at Shakopee donated their blood to the American Red Cross.

Even before World War II ended, America started to return to the way things had been before the war, and so did Shakopee. Anthony Cottage reopened on February 1, 1945. Six weeks later, Clara Thune replaced Estelle Jamieson and became Shakopee's fourth superintendent.

Clara Thune arrived at Shakopee with nearly 20 years of experience in the courts and criminal justice system. She had served as a clerk of probate and juvenile court while also acting as a probation officer for juvenile girls and handling aid to dependent children cases. Like her predecessors she had no previous experience working in a correctional facility.

During her 14 years at Shakopee, Superintendent Thune was credited with making a number of changes that improved conditions for the inmates. Some of the rules were relaxed if not removed, and the women were given more freedom of choice with such things as hair care, use of cosmetics and clothing allowances. But the most important contributions that Clara Thune made during her years as superintendent hinged upon her ability to say "Yes" to someone else's good idea and her willingness to give the women at Shakopee the opportunity to rise to the occasion.

Following World War II the state faced a growing problem with overcrowding in its facilities for retarded children. The legislature responded in 1951 by designating Shaw Cottage as the Shakopee Home for Children. The cottage was remodeled to house 30 children, and on September 19, 1951, Shaw Cottage received its new tenants. As a result Superintendent Thune had two administrative hats to wear.

The children who were sent to Shakopee were all girls between the ages of four and twelve; they were classified as untrainable and were to receive only custodial care. A staff of ten transferred with the children and they were joined by an equal number of inmate assistants. The combination of staff and inmates provided the children with an exceptionally caring environment. The program was beneficial for both the children and the inmates. It wasn't long before the program at Shakopee was being cited as "unique in providing a program of rehabilitation which has a humanitarian aspect." Children who were once considered completely helpless were learning various simple tasks because of the excellent care they were receiving.

In the spring 1964 issue of the *Reflector*, one of the inmates who was working with the retarded children wrote an article entitled "The Home Has Helped Me." Carla wrote: "When I go to work, it is a dream come true. To someone I am very, very important. It is not important to these retarded children that I committed a crime. It is important that I can wipe away tears and kiss a cut…that makes me feel very special. And that is how the 'home' has helped me."

In the spring 1965 issue of the *Reflector*, an inmate reported how the children were responding: "The girls can tie their shoes, wash their hands, do a dance, color a picture, play ball, say a name, and even smile in a certain way." Even more help was on the way.

In 1966 a three-year federal grant was used to hire Donald Hanson to direct the program for the retarded children and to train staff in new methods to be used to teach the children basic skills. Mrs. Richard Westphal, a volunteer who visited the children at Shakopee, commented on the effects of the new program: "The change since Mr. Hanson has been in charge has really been wonderful to watch. The personal involvement of the women from the reformatory has always been very strong, and the children always had the benefit of more love and affection there than they could get anywhere else. But since the women have been shown how to train the girls, the children have really picked up a lot in the things they can do."

The children's lives were richer and the inmates were doing good work, but in 1969, after more than 17 years at Shakopee, the Department of Welfare didn't need the space that Shaw Cottage provided. The number of mentally retarded patients in state institutions had declined. The fact that the program was good for the inmates as well as the children was not a factor in the decision. The Children's Home at Shakopee was closed on June 30, 1969. At the time the superintendent observed, "A real asset to the reformatory is leaving. It has done the inmates tremendous psychological and emotional good to work with these children – someone who needs them and isn't judging them."

Clara Thune's other "Yes" helped to create the Braille Project, probably the most amazing volunteer effort that inmates at Shakopee were ever involved in. It began in 1955 with an inquiry from Services for the Blind to the Supervisor of Corrections regarding the possibility of inmates doing braille transcription as a work assignment. The following year, Services for the Blind contacted Mrs. Joseph Bonoff and discussed the idea with her. She turned to the Sisterhood of Temple Israel, seeking their help in starting a braille transcription project with the women at Shakopee. The Supervisor of Corrections and Superintendent Clara Thune worked out the administrative details and invited inmates to volunteer for training. Five women volunteered and began the course in braille transcription under the supervision of Mrs. Bonoff.

In June 1956, four of the women completed their training and were awarded certificates as "Volunteer Braille Transcribers" from the Library of Congress. Superintendent Thune was given a gold pin with six diamonds for her role in establishing the braille department at Shakopee. It was the only prison in the country with such a program.

Soon the women at Shakopee were transcribing thousands of pages of reading material. During the year from July 1, 1958, to June 30, 1959, seven inmate braillists transcribed more than 35,000 pages of text. Included in this output were 55 textbooks that ranged in subject matter from Aristotle to phonics and psychology. Requests for work came from as far away as China. The Braille Project was a morale builder for the women transcribers and a positive factor in their rehabilitation.

In 1959 five women earned Braille Certificates and pins, Mary Jo received a "Meritorious" pin for brailling 10,000 pages, and Viola received a "Distinguished Service" pin for reaching 20,000 pages. Between 1956 and 1959, a total of 13 women were certified by the Library of Congress.

In 1963 the Braille Project inmate supervisor reported in the *Reflector* that one of the braillists at Shakopee had set a record for the State of Minnesota by brailling 220 pages of text in one week. The women in the Braille Project added new dimensions to their work by learning braille bookbinding and duplicating.

Joyce, a braillist with the project, wrote in the *Reflector* about the pride that they had in the blind students they had helped with the textbooks they transcribed. She named John J. Boyer, who majored in mathematics and psychology at St. Thomas College in St. Paul. He graduated second highest in his class and was awarded a scholarship to Notre Dame. Another blind student, Craig R. Anderson, graduated from Carleton College in Northfield and was given an "Outstanding Achievement Award" by President Lyndon Johnson.

In 1965 the average daily population at Shakopee fell to 49 women; for the next two years the average daily population was 46 women. The Braille Project faltered and the duplicating part of the project was shut down in 1966. By 1970 the Braille Project was gone, but not finished.

In 1991 long-term inmates were invited to be trained in brailling. Four women volunteered, but only Donna completed the training and was certified. For the next ten years Donna continued to transcribe texts into braille. She made several attempts to train other women, but none completed the training. When Donna left Shakopee in 2001, the Braille Project closed for the second time. Through the Braille Project women inmates at Shakopee gave more than 20 years of service to the blind.

On May 24, 1957, Clara Thune honored several state employees at Shakopee. One was Mr. Nick Thilgen, who was the farm supervisor for 37 years from March 23, 1920, until his retirement on April 11, 1957. He received a gold pin in the shape of the State of Minnesota, a lightweight jacket from the staff and after-shave lotion from the Children's Home employees. In the years that followed Mr. Thilgen's retirement, portions of the 160-acre farm were sold to the City of Shakopee, Scott County, and St. Mark's Cemetery. The 36 acres of land that were retained from the original farm became the site for the new institution.

In October 1958, Ruby Benson began her career at Shakopee as the assistant superintendent. She was a graduate of St. Olaf College in Northfield and had done graduate studies in social work at the University of Minnesota. She had more than 20 years of experience as a social worker, first with the Federal Emergency Relief Administration (F.E.R.A.) beginning in 1934, and then as a field representative with the State Department of Welfare from 1938 to 1958.

When Ruby Benson became superintendent on July 15, 1959, she was well acquainted with the inmates, the staff, the programs and the issues that the reformatory faced. Like Clara Thune, Superintendent Benson wore two administrative hats: one for the Reformatory and one for the Children's Home. Ruby Benson was appointed by Morris Hursh, the Commissioner of Public Welfare, but she was soon reporting to the first Commissioner of Corrections, Will C. Turnbladh.

Ruby Benson was the last superintendent to live in the superintendent's apartment in Isabel Higbee Hall, and she was the last to be on duty 24 hours a day, seven days a week. Ruby was called upon to guide Shakopee through some difficult transition years.

The fall 1959 issue of the *Reflector* was very kind to Superintendent Clara Thune and gave her credit for "many penal reforms . . . which have set this Reformatory out in front as a leader in modern penology." The words echoed the praise that the Reflector gave to Superintendent Jamieson in 1938.

The *Reflector* went on to warmly welcome the new superintendent and said that Ruby Benson was "a very special person" who "wears well" and plays life "straight." The article also noted her understanding of human nature, offered the hope that Ruby Benson would serve for many years and would add her accomplishments "to those of Isabel Higbee and Clara Thune." High hopes, perhaps, but with good reason.

Ruby Benson's first few years were marked with a number of successes. The Braille Project was flourishing. The Children's Home was good for the children as well as the inmates. By the summer of 1961, ten women were working in the Braille Project and ten in the Children's Home. On June 4, 1961, Ruby Benson was awarded The Distinguished Alumnus Award by St. Olaf College.

The summer 1962 issue of the *Reflector* praised Superintendent Benson for improving the inmate rule book. It went on to applaud the rule change that allowed women to play their radios until 10:30 p.m., cited the courses in Slimnastics and personal development, and the volunteer service. The paper shared Miss Benson's hopes for an occupational therapist who would teach arts and crafts, a full time chaplain, and improved psychiatric services.

In the fall of 1962, Tai Shigaki joined the Shakopee staff as assistant superintendent. Tai was part of a growing wave of corrections administrators who had earned master's degrees in social work. She joined Superintendent Benson in developing rehabilitation programs for the inmates and formal training for the staff. At the time there were 33 staff members at Shakopee; ten were working with the children in Shaw Cottage, and 23 were working with the 58 adult women in the reformatory.

Some rough times were coming. The inmate population began to decline. The average daily population dropped to 54 in 1963, 51 in 1964, 49 in 1965, 46 in 1966, and 46 in 1967. There was talk of closing Shakopee or moving to a different location.

The fact that Shakopee had no perimeter wall or fence began to be a concern to area residents. In March 1964, The Shakopee City Council voted unanimously in favor of a resolution requesting that "the State of Minnesota install an enclosure around the Shakopee State Reformatory for Women." The vote followed an incident in which a 19-year-old inmate escaped from the institution and, armed with a butcher knife, entered a residence where she threatened two children. The children were unharmed, and the inmate surrendered and was returned to the institution within 25 minutes.

Speaking for the Department of Corrections, Deputy Commissioner Howard Costello stated that a fence was not sufficient to keep people in an institution "unless you have a barbed wire enclosure with gun towers." He went on to say, "That would defeat the entire purpose of the institution. One of its goals is to give the women a sense of responsibility, to let them live in as normal an atmosphere as possible." The matter was dropped for the moment.

Ruby Benson hired Irene Powers in 1964 as a substitute for a full time cottage staff member who was scheduled to take two weeks vacation. Irene worked upstairs in Higbee. She thought the job would be temporary. Twenty years later in 1984, Irene Powers retired. When she was hired, she was called a house parent, and when she retired, she was called a correctional counselor. Her career mirrors the transition that Shakopee went through. Irene Powers' memories and reflections help to illuminate those years.

Irene began working on June 14, 1964, as a house parent for $285 per month. As a house parent, she was on duty 24 hours per day, but she was not paid for the hours from 10:00 p.m. to 6:00 a.m. when she could sleep if there were no disturbances. Her days began at 7:00 a.m. when she and the other house parents went from door to door in their cottages and knocked on the women's doors to get them up.

The inmates lived a regimented life. "Like the army," Irene Powers said. The women wore print dresses to all meals. Breakfast was at 8:00 a.m. After breakfast, the women returned to their rooms to change into their work clothes. For work, most women wore coveralls, light blue dresses that were like muumuus. They went to sewing, housekeeping, braille, the school, the kitchen, the laundry, the garden, and grounds keeping from 8:30 to 11:30 a.m. Then they went back to their rooms, where they changed back into their print dresses for lunch. They waited on the stairways in their cottages from 11:55 to 12:00 noon when their house parent rang the lunch bell. After lunch, the women changed back into their coveralls and they could watch "As the World Turns" on TV until 1:00 p.m. Then it was back to work from 1:00 to 4:00 p.m. At 4:00 p.m. the women returned to their rooms for baths, and personal hygiene. At 5:00 p.m. it was time for supper in the print dresses once again. From 6:00 to 8:30 p.m. the women could watch TV, and many did some kind of sewing or knitting. Women could have one cigarette after each meal and one final cigarette at 8:00 p.m. At 8:30 p.m. the women went to their rooms. "Lights off" was at 9:00 p.m.

Although life in the institution was very regimented during the 1960s, Irene Powers gave Ruby Benson high marks as superintendent. "She was really a nice person...very caring," Irene said. Ruby was very supportive of her staff and although she could not always solve their problems, "She would always listen."

Ruby Benson found herself looking for a good secretary in 1965, and she had the good fortune to find Darlene Peterson. Darlene was the first secretary to the superintendent who did not live at the institution. Darlene and her husband had a home in Shakopee, so the requirement to live at the institution was dropped. Apparently Darlene's work was more than satisfactory; she retired in 1991 after serving three superintendents.

Darlene recalled how the administrative staff ate lunch together with the superintendent in a formal dining room in Higbee Hall. The table was set with linen tablecloths and napkins in napkin holders. Each staff member had an assigned place, and an inmate served as their waitress. Superintendent Benson taught Darlene all the procedures for her job as secretary which included the admission paperwork that was done with each new inmate. Darlene also typed up the medical and psychiatric reports for the institution, and as a result she developed an extensive knowledge of issues relating to the lives of women in prison.

Like many people who have worked in prisons or reformatories, Darlene Peterson came to the conclusion that some inmates should not be in prison, but rather should be receiving appropriate care or treatment in a mental hospital or other facility. Unfortunately, the staff at Shakopee found that if they could get an inmate sent to St. Peter State Hospital, "They would send her back in two weeks," Darlene said.

On August 29, 1966, four inmates from Sanford Cottage took their house parent hostage and escaped with her in her own car. They made it safely to Minneapolis. Once again the area residents wondered if the neighborhood might be safer with a fence around the reformatory. The Department of Corrections responded as it had in the past by pointing out that the type of fence that appealed to the neighbors would not deter escapes. The matter was dropped.

On Thursday, June 26, 1969, the Shakopee *Valley News* reported that Ruby Benson was going to retire on the following Wednesday, July 2. It went on to note that her retirement would coincide almost exactly with the closing of the Children's Home at the institution. The Children's Home was scheduled to close two days earlier on June 30.

The article mentioned that Miss Benson "was visibly saddened as she spoke about the imminent closing of the facility for the retarded." But she was careful to point out that Shaw Cottage was not designed to be used as a children's facility, and other changes made closing it a practical move.

Although it appeared that her life-long career of social work was coming to a close on a sad note, Superintendent Benson was philosophical about her career: "I just hope that somewhere along the line I've been able to help someone."

When Ruby Benson retired, she reflected upon the fact that throughout her years with the Department of Corrections, rehabilitation of prisoners had always been the goal, but the effort had changed from "a hope or ideal into a concentrated all-out attempt to salvage the lives of such people." At Shakopee, she noted, "There has been much more emphasis on treatment – psychological, vocational training – everything we can do to equip the women to live a normal life and make a go of it according to the rules of society."

Although Shakopee was a small institution with an inmate population of less than 60 at that time, the professional staff included a part-time psychiatrist, a part-time psychologist, a full time accredited teacher, a resident corrections agent, and two social workers (including Ruby Benson). During nearly all of her tenure, Superintendent Benson was also in charge of the home for retarded children that cared for 30 young girls in Shaw Cottage. She noted that many more professional people were being trained as treatment staff – not custodial staff. During the next 25 years, the movement toward greater efforts in the treatment and rehabilitation of inmates would continue.

What Ruby Benson said was an "all-out attempt to salvage the lives" of men and women in prison may have been an over statement, but she was witnessing a growing effort to provide rehabilitative programming. Commissioner Paul W. Keve was one of the agents of that change as was his Deputy Commissioner, Howard Costello. When Ruby Benson announced her intention to retire, Mr. Keve and Mr. Costello considered possible candidates who could be expected to carry the program forward. Robert Bergherr was their choice.

Robert Bergherr was born in Morris, Minnesota, in 1928. Following high school, he joined the Marines and served in the Pacific. He graduated from the College of St. Thomas with a bachelor's degree in sociology and spent nearly 12 years in field services as a parole and probation officer. Bergherr earned a master's of social work from the University of Minnesota in 1962 and became the Director of Thistledew Forestry Camp, working with young male offenders. Prior to being appointed superintendent at Shakopee, Mr. Bergherr also worked as director of field services, as a school social worker, and as an assistant professor of social work at the University of Minnesota.

The summer 1969 issue of the *Reflector* was interesting in several ways. It contained a final article from Ruby Benson entitled "Across the Superintendent's Desk," in which she praised the volunteer program at Shakopee, the six men and 18 women who assisted with activities that ranged from group therapy and AA meetings to Bible study, tutoring, charm class, and gym. There was no farewell from the superintendent, but there were several articles and a poem written by inmates that acknowledged her retirement, and the editor reflected upon how much better life was at Shakopee in 1969 than it had been in 1959.

In the same issue, Commissioner Paul Keve authored an article entitled "Does Corrections Have a Future?" He wrote about the artificial nature of life in prison and the movement toward "more realistic living for prisoners." He went on to say, "Perhaps at Shakopee in the years ahead, we will have a chance of trying some new ways of giving more meaningful and real-life experiences." He then expressed his pleasure in having Mr. Bergherr as the new Superintendent.

Commissioner Keve concluded by paying his respects to Ruby Benson for her years of service. "She has brought to her work gentle, genuine and humane regard for people," he wrote. "She deserves our warmest good wishes for an enjoyable retirement."

The Commissioner's article was followed by one entitled "Your New Superintendent" by Deputy Commissioner Howard Costello. It began by expressing regret at losing Ruby Benson, and continued by welcoming Robert Bergherr. It cited his education, military service, work experience and family. The torch was passed to the next generation.

Just over 40 years of age, Superintendent Bergherr quickly achieved several firsts. He was the first man to serve as superintendent, and the first to live off grounds. He and his family lived in Bloomington. He was the first superintendent to have children, and the first who did not work 24 hours per day. Although like other wardens and superintendents, he could be called upon at any time in an emergency.

The fall 1969 issue of the *Reflector* reported what the new superintendent had on his agenda. He was searching for an assistant superintendent; he would hire Pat Davis who had earned his master's of social work from Tulane. Bergherr was setting up a new point system with the hope that it would be a better measuring device for the Parole Board to use as they attempted to evaluate when inmates were ready for parole. He was setting up a court of review so that inmates could appeal discipline decisions. He was starting up a data processing vocational program in the basement of Shaw Cottage using keypunch equipment. And, finally, Superintendent Bergherr was ready to begin an independent living program for women preparing for release by housing them in the apartment in Higbee that had been used by past superintendents.

The paper also reported that the education program was flourishing. Office skills equipment had just arrived: typewriters, business machines, and a multilith machine. Some women were taking academic correspondence courses from St. Cloud Reformatory. Ten women were taking correspondence courses from the University of Minnesota, and an Augsburg College professor was bringing a criminology class to Shakopee for fall quarter.

The professor was Cal Appleby. He brought not only the criminology course, but also one half of the class–12 Augsburg students. The other half of the class were 12 women at Shakopee. It was the beginning of a wonderful symbiotic relationship with Augsburg. Two years later Augsburg's Vern Bloom expanded the program using federal funds and the cooperation of Augsburg College. It was a good experience for the Augsburg students to learn that women in prison could succeed in college classes just as they could, and it confirmed in the women what they could achieve if they believed in themselves. The relationship between Augsburg and Shakopee continued for nearly 30 years.

Robert Bergherr found that working with women was different from working with men as he had at Thistledew or on parole. He felt that the women were more deceptive than men, perhaps more seductive also, but he had no serious problems. Once an inmate picked up a pair of scissors from his desk in a threatening manner, but she put them down when he told her to. He had a high regard for the staff at Shakopee. Even though most were not professionally trained, he said they were "trained to be caring and considerate and kind." They did a lot of listening and developed "a good intimate knowledge" of the women at Shakopee.

Looking back on his year as superintendent, Mr. Bergherr felt he received adequate support from Central Office, and he remembered attending the monthly meetings with the other CEOs of the adult institutions. He appreciated the help he got from the institution nurse in creating the shift work schedules, and he remembered Florence Hanson, the business manager, who was a powerful guardian of the state's money. However, Robert Bergherr and Shakopee were not well matched. He was more at home with counseling or school social work, and Shakopee needed a superintendent who was focused on creating the conditions that the women needed: self esteem, hope, and a new beginning.

Commissioner Paul Keve may have had the wrong person in the job at Shakopee, but he was sure that he wanted a superintendent who was professionally trained in the field of social work. One of his former students was working in California. He visited her there and suggested that she consider returning to Minnesota. After 20 years as a social worker, mental health counselor, administrator, and child welfare advocate, Jackie Fleming was ready to come home.

In 1970 a new era began at Shakopee, the Fleming years. No one could have known that Jackie Fleming was about to spend her next 22 years at Shakopee. When she retired in 1992, more than 30 per cent of Shakopee's history would be her story also.

She signed her name D. Jacqueline Fleming, but everyone called her Jackie. She had just turned 43 when she began her years as Shakopee's seventh superintendent. At five feet five inches, she was not imposing physically, but she had a special presence. Her dark hair was beginning to streak with gray, her eyes were bright, and she laughed easily. Compared to the other superintendents, she was most like Florence Monahan, having "a modern outlook, a solid training, a deep interest in women and children, and...health and enthusiasm."

Jackie Fleming began her new life as superintendent on October 5, 1970. Within a few weeks the Minneapolis *Tribune* did an article about her entitled "Woman Warden Works for Change." It had two sub-headlines, "More Training Programs Needed" and "Warden: 'Staff Needs Men.'" Marg Zack, the *Tribune* reporter, captured the major themes that Jackie Fleming would develop during the next 22 years. She quoted Jackie as saying, "It's hard to say what a prison should be...Corrections institutions are in somewhat the same spot as mental institutions. The public doesn't like to be reminded they're needed."

Like the first superintendent, Fleming had no background in corrections. She began by learning about the institution, analyzing programs, and thinking about changes that needed to be made. She felt that the inmates needed to take more responsibility for their own lives. Jackie would initiate an inmate council and involve inmates and staff in reviewing the institution rules.

Jackie was bright and well educated with a bachelor's degree in sociology and history from St. Olaf College and a master's in social work from the University of Minnesota. Her 20 years of experience in social work and mental health prepared her to rekindle the embers of rehabilitation programming at Shakopee.

In order to improve community relations and public awareness of the institution, she proposed having a community advisory board. The women also needed "training programs and maybe some kind of industry." From her social work and mental health background, Fleming knew that "Many women have had bad experiences with men and need a positive male image." Hiring more men on the institution staff would be a way to help the women at Shakopee develop more positive attitudes about men.

Like the early 1920s, the 1970s supported and encouraged the belief that rehabilitation was desirable for women in prison. The leadership of the Department of Corrections supported the changes that Jackie introduced, or at least were willing to let her try. She was able to argue that women needed to be treated differently from the way men were being treated at Stillwater. The commissioner's response was pretty much that as long as there weren't adverse reports in the newspapers, Jackie could make the changes she wanted. She believed that the women needed to deal with the issues in their lives: low self-esteem, grief, abuse, chemical dependency, and the need to develop skills in communications, parenting, relationships, education and job skills. Jackie felt that when a woman was sent to prison, that was the punishment. What happened in prison should prepare the woman to return to society.

To achieve those goals Jackie Fleming needed help from the right people. Some of the right people were already at Shakopee. One was Pat Davis, the assistant superintendent that Jackie inherited from the previous administration. Another was Darlene Peterson, who helped Jackie with shift schedules and staff evaluations in addition to her secretarial duties. A third person was Irene Powers, who began as a substitute house parent and continued as a valuable staff member for 20 years.

In the spring 1971 issue of the *Reflector*, Jackie wrote, "My primary long-term goal is to provide an institution which will enable every woman to learn something to better prepare her to return to society and live a meaningful, productive life." She wanted to create an environment of mutual respect and trust that would provide the women with opportunities to develop their self-esteem and to learn and to grow.

The Land of the Dragon helped do exactly that. When Professor Burt Meisel volunteered his services to direct Shakopee women in putting on a play that would be performed at Mankato State College, Jackie not only agreed, but she also provided the leadership that led to success. *The Land of the Dragon* was a tremendous undertaking for 24 women in prison to learn the roles and perform a play five times to audiences of 600 on a stage 50 miles away from Shakopee. This was a test of trust and mutual respect, and it was a great self-esteem builder. Back and forth they traveled on their yellow school bus, Old Yeller. Old Yeller performed almost as well as the women, breaking down only once during the June 4-6 performance trips.

When the performances were over, everyone seemed pleased. As a reward to the women involved in the play, Jackie Fleming threw a beach party at her family cabin on Bass Lake at Annandale on June 13. Old Yeller transported the 24 women. Jackie, her mom, four staff, two spouses and a neighbor hosted the party which included swimming, boating, fishing, and lots of fun and good food. Like the play, the party was a big success.

It was evident that Jackie, her staff and the women were creating a new environment, something better than before. In the fall 1971 issue of the *Reflector*, Jackie wrote about what "we" had accomplished and about respect, trust and esteem building. She concluded, "...this has been one of the more rewarding years of my life."

Jackie Fleming had very little money to spend on fixing the deteriorating buildings or to spend on hiring new staff, but she had success in California using volunteers to provide needed programming. She asked around to find an exceptional person to create an expanded volunteer program. When Jackie found Ricky Littlefield, she struck gold.

Ricky, a well-educated New Yorker transplanted to the Lake Minnetonka area, was the second vice president of the Junior League. She got a call from Jackie in November. It took nearly a year for Jackie to convince Ricky that she should volunteer to become the Volunteer Coordinator for Shakopee. Ricky's basic job was to get volunteers to help create the programming that the women needed. Equally important was the need to create the programs, set criteria, lay out plans, and organize.

Years later Ricky said in an interview, "Jackie had a belief in the women and in the possibilities in people. Jackie empowered people; she had no stereotypes, everything was a possibility." And Ricky, with her Junior League experience to bolster her, was ready to change possibilities into realities.

The Off Grounds Vocational Program was Ricky's first big project. She teamed up with Pat Davis who had written a grant to fund a program that would allow women to go off grounds full time to school or work in the community. Eventually as many as ten inmates went off grounds to school or to various work sites in the Shakopee area and beyond. Local women were hired to drive inmates to and from worksites that included Como Park Zoo in St. Paul and Friendship Manor, a nursing home in Shakopee. The women in the Off Grounds Vocational Program were eventually housed together in Shaw Cottage that was designated as the honor unit.

Ricky was good at grant writing and stretching resources; Jackie was good at empowering staff and was willing to try new ideas. Turning volunteers into "custody volunteers" was another of their good ideas that worked.

The idea was to provide volunteers with sufficient security training so that they could competently take women off grounds to attend to things that ranged from medical appointments to funerals. At the men's institutions, correctional officers usually provided these services, but Shakopee did not have sufficient staff to satisfy the inmates' needs. Before long Ricky had 65 custody volunteers providing service to the inmates and protecting public safety at the same time. Jackie and Ricky had faith in the volunteers and in the inmates. They expected the inmates to respond in a positive way, and the inmates rarely let them down. Ricky said, "If I would go the extra mile for the inmate, she would go the extra mile for me."

Jackie also thought that the women needed a chance to speak up, so she started an inmate council made up of inmate representatives elected by the women in their living units. Some staff objected to treating the inmates so well, but Superintendent Fleming got her way. She chaired the regular meetings of the inmate council until she retired.

Being well groomed was important to Jackie Fleming; one indication was her own hair appointment at a local beauty shop every Monday afternoon. She knew that the women felt better about themselves when they were well groomed also, so she allowed them to have hair care products, a place to do their hair, and greater freedom in wearing make-up. Additionally, a local beautician was allowed to make regular visits to the institution, and the women paid for her services with money they had earned through their work.

Jackie also reformed the dress code by allowing greater choice in what the women were allowed to wear and the number of articles of clothing they could have in their possession. Some women were escorted off grounds to shop for clothing. Many women ordered clothes from department store catalogs. All of the women were able to shop for free at the Boutique, a used clothing shop housed in a room at the institution and supplied with clothes gathered by local churchwomen. Naturally, rules were created that determined what clothing was allowed and what was not and how much was enough. Compared to the men's institutions, the clothing allowances for the women at Shakopee were extremely generous, but male staff members who knew about this discrepancy were wise to stay out of the discussions when women staff decided how much clothing was enough.

Ricky Littlefield and others continued to write grants and develop group therapy programs dealing with grief, self-esteem, chemical dependency, and parenting. To an outside observer the parenting program was the one that turned heads and was most innovative.

In the early 1970s Jackie Fleming began allowing women to have their children stay overnight on weekends as a way to help the women and children stay connected, but there were problems. It became evident that most of the inmate mothers were lacking in parenting skills, so Jackie turned to Ricky Littlefield, who wrote a federal grant proposal requesting LEAA funds. The proposal for a parenting program was accepted and a three-year program was funded. Once again Shakopee needed the right person; Ricky found Patt Adair.

Patt had been working in the Wilder Foundation's early childhood education program in St. Paul's Selby-Dale neighborhood and teaching parenting in the community. When Ricky first contacted Patt and said that they wanted to start a parenting program at Shakopee, Patt's initial answer was "no thanks." But Ricky persisted and invited Patt to visit Shakopee where she met with Ricky and Jackie Fleming. The meeting went well for Shakopee. Patt said later, "I found it a fascinating idea."

Patt began in October 1977. She had "pretty much a free hand" in creating the program. Since parenting education was relatively new, there were no national models, but curriculum was being developed in the local community. At Shakopee, Patt combined parent education classes for the women during the week with structured activities for the women and their children on the weekends. "What became ultimately clear to me," Patt recalled, "is that these mothers had never really played themselves, so they didn't know the behaviors to model. They didn't really know what to do with their kids. And as it turned out, the women had as much fun as the kids." The women got involved in lots of activities including finger painting and making play dough, things that they had never done before. The women were enjoying themselves and their children, they were learning things that they could do with their children, and they were learning how to structure their time. Patt also taught the inmate moms the right words to use when disciplining their children and how to help their children develop self-esteem.

The parenting program produced several additional benefits. First, the parenting group sessions became safe places for the women to discuss painful issues in their own lives including the abuse they suffered as children. Secondly, the collective behavior of the women in the institution improved on the weekends when the children were present. Patt Adair recalled, "...the women behaved much better on weekends when the kids were there. Everybody rose to the occasion."

Eventually, Patt helped to plan the parenting program that would be developed in the new facility that was completed in 1986. The group room and its connected children's room with child-size tables and chairs, the women's beds with trundle beds built in for use by children on weekends, and the outdoor play area for children indicated the commitment that was being made to helping women and their children survive the trauma of incarceration. No prison ever seemed more humane than the new institution on a Saturday at noon in the food service dining room when women and their children could be seen enjoying lunch together as families.

In November 1977, about a month after Patt Adair began the parenting program, Ricky Littlefield interviewed Shirley Shumate to head the chemical dependency program. Shirley had recently completed the Chemical Dependency Specialist program at Minneapolis Community College, and like Patt, she had no intention of working in a prison. But that changed after she had met with Ricky. When Ricky offered her the job, Shirley accepted.

Shirley Shumate was responsible for developing and running the chemical dependency program. She set up a program that combined individual counseling and group sessions. The groups had a maximum of 12 women and ran for 12 weeks. In the beginning, the group sessions were held in Higbee in the area that had been the superintendent's apartment. When the women completed the 12-week program, they had a graduation ceremony.

Recalling the graduation ceremonies, Shirley said, "In the early years, they were quite the production." There was a program with entertainment and refreshments. Outside guests came, and so did spouses and children. In the new institution, graduations were held in food service, a very attractive room, nicely furnished and full of color.

Shirley was hired under an LEAA grant that Ricky had written, and Ricky informed Shirley that if she wanted to keep her program going, she would have to write the next grant application. Shirley did. Eventually, she was able to get acupuncture treatments added to the program. When surveyed, about 75 per cent of the women felt that acupuncture was helpful to them.

Shirley credited Jackie Fleming for many good ideas including the use of acupuncture. "She was my mentor," Shirley said in a recent interview. "The older I get, the more I admire her for what she did."

In 1986 Barb Landoe went to Shakopee hoping to intern in the chemical dependency program. She met with Shirley Shumate, who didn't know until then that she needed an intern. After the meeting Shirley decided that Barb would be a good addition to the program, and for the next five years they provided most of the chemical dependency programming at Shakopee.

Because funds were short, Barb actually worked first as a driver and then as a correctional officer at Shakopee until she could become a full time partner with Shirley in the chemical dependency program. Looking back, Barb Landoe said that those years with Shirley Shumate were "the best of times... when the state believed in rehabilitation." Shirley Shumate left Shakopee in 1991 and continued to be an advocate for women's programs.

Barb continued to run the program and was joined by other correctional program therapists (CPTs). Eventually, Anthony living unit was designated as the treatment unit. Barb became the Director but soon found that overseeing 16 correctional officers and three CPTs didn't leave her with much time and energy to be involved in the actual therapy program.

Barb was able to step down, but she never again felt the sense of accomplishment that she had when she and Shirley Shumate worked together.

As the inmate population increased, procedures became more like those in the men's institutions. More paperwork was required, and staff turnover made everything more difficult. Barb was reassigned to work with women in Meade, the mental health unit. Barb continued to work there until her retirement in 2000.

After the schoolteacher resigned in June 1972, Jackie Fleming took the opportunity to add a man to her staff and improve the education program. She hired Roger Knudson, who had been teaching juvenile males at St. Croix Camp. Roger was married and had a seven-year-old son. He liked running, biking, and making furniture. He became a good male role model for the women.

As a teacher Roger Knudson could see that his work was cut out for him. In September when he arrived, there was no education program in operation. The classroom/library space in the basement of Higbee was small. There were ten typewriters lined up on a large table, five on each side. There were typing and shorthand books, but little else. An inmate librarian named Sharon shared the space that Roger hoped to use as a classroom. When he entered the area on his first day, Sharon asked, "What do you think you're doing here?" It was his first test. Five and a half years later, Sharon wrote an article in the *Reflector* entitled "The Man Who Invaded My Privacy." In the article, she recounted that first meeting and how she resented his intrusion, but within three weeks he had won her over, and during the intervening years he did many good things for the education program and the women at Shakopee.

Jackie Fleming, however, was very open to Roger's ideas and she encouraged him to be creative. She hoped that he might involve as many as half of the women in education programs. He soon learned that the women's needs and desires ranged from basic literacy to high school/GED programming to vocational and college level classes. Although some educational programming had been going on at Shakopee since the very beginning, Roger's mandate was to do more and to do it better. Roger was pleased with the strong support he received from Jackie Fleming and from her assistant, Pat Davis, but he was disappointed when Mr. Davis left Shakopee shortly after Roger was hired.

Roger enjoyed working with the women, and he found them very challenging. He worked hard to establish a good reputation with them and found that once he had, his work with the inmates went much more smoothly. Apparently, the word spread that he was "OK," and he was spared additional testing behavior.

Providing a wide range of educational programs to a relatively small population was very challenging. Shakopee lacked the economies of scale that a large institution like Stillwater enjoyed, yet the women had a right to the educational opportunities that were available to the men. Roger used individualized instruction and correspondence courses as much as he could. He was able to get help on a part-time basis from Mary Strand, an excellent literacy teacher, and from Carol Buesgens, a correctional officer. He was open to alternative education programs like those of Gwen Jones Davis and Antioch Communiversity that had flourished for a few years in North Minneapolis.

Roger Knudson developed a good relationship with Ron Ward, an administrator with the Shakopee public schools. Ron loaned some Apple computers to Roger for a summer, and before long Roger developed a network using a Corvus system. With the network Roger was able to serve a number of inmates a variety of subjects at different grade levels all at the same time. He even placed an Apple computer in Higbee's segregation unit and connected it to the Corvus network so that women there could keep on learning.

Roger continued to be bothered by how difficult it was to provide small numbers of students with college or vocational classes. Then he talked to Bill Leto at Hennepin Technical College, and they developed the vision that two-way interactive TV could connect women at Shakopee to classes at HTC. It would take several years. The education area moved "across the street" to the new building in 1986, and Roger left Shakopee a few months later, but his vision eventually became a reality.

Eight years earlier in 1978, the climate of public opinion appeared to be changing toward Shakopee and efforts to provide rehabilitation. In an article in the Minneapolis *Star*, Debra Stone wrote, "The era of reform has come and gone." The Shakopee City Council passed a resolution in September 1978 asking that the institution put up a ten- foot high chain-link fence topped with barbed wire. In the recent past, several women convicted of violent crimes had been sent to Shakopee. Perhaps the most infamous was Jean who was found guilty of the murder of a 22 year old woman and her two children. A newspaper article described the crime: "The three victims had been wired to a bed and their apartment had been set afire. (She) was accused of buying gasoline used in the fire and of driving David M. Olson to the apartment to set the blaze."

Shakopee was experiencing nine or ten escapes per year. The prison was overcrowded and in need of repair. Bars had been put on all the windows, but there were only two maximum-security cells. Early in December 1978, two women sawed through window bars and escaped.

Jackie Fleming said, "Somebody, somehow, in this state is going to have to decide what's going to be done with women. I feel that eventually a new facility is going to be needed – a more secure facility, possibly with a fence around it."

The legislature considered several options. Moving the women to Rochester was considered because the state hospital was scheduled for closing, and 450 jobs would be lost. It was estimated that a move to renovated buildings in Rochester would cost four to five million dollars, whereas building a replacement institution at Shakopee would cost $13 million. The discussions continued.

Eventually, Corrections Commissioner Jack Young recommended on February 3, 1982, that the Shakopee location be retained for a number of reasons including the good of the inmates. On April 20,1983, the Shakopee *Valley News* announced that Governor Perpich was in support of the recommendation made by Commissioner Orville Pung for a $15 million institution. The legislature agreed and the planning began in earnest. The new institution would be built on the 36 acres of land that remained from the original 160-acre farm across the street on Sixth Avenue.

Jim Zellmer, the Director of Institutional Support Services, was assigned as the project director for building the new institution. He represented the Department of Corrections and was the connecting link between the staff at Shakopee, the department, the architects, and the contractors. Mr. Zellmer had been the department's project director for the construction of Oak Park

Heights a few years earlier. He took pride in the planning process he used at Shakopee and in the final results. He said later, "What we set out to do, we accomplished."

Jim developed a planning guide that he called "the red book." It divided the institution into its component parts: administration, security, education, programs, industry, food service, and living units. Staff members were taken off grounds in small groups to discuss the various components. They were asked questions about their roles in the institution as well as their immediate needs and future needs.

Although Jim Zellmer felt Jackie Fleming was worried that he wanted to create an Oak Park Heights for women, he assured her that this was not his intention. Jackie and her staff were very much part of the planning process. What Jim called a "campus concept" was developed for the new institution. It had as its main focus accommodating the women's needs. There would be greater security, but there would be no fence. There would be carpeting, soft furniture, lots of windows, small courtyards, good lighting and color. In the core building there would be a "main street" hallway with education, programs, chapel, health services, art room, gym, and food service all easily accessible. The three regular living units would house 32 inmates, still small and homey, each with a small kitchen and good storage space.

The plan anticipated the presence of children in the institution. Each woman's bed would have a trundle bed built beneath it that could be used by a child. A children's room with child-size chairs, tables, and sink would be built next to the group room. The two rooms would be connected to a small kitchen. A children's play area would be part of the main courtyard.

Some ideas were gathered from visits to other states. The Independent Living Center (ILC) was modeled on an Arkansas Department of Corrections women's facility, but it also allowed ideas to bloom that began in Higbee's apartment and Shaw Cottage. The ILC seemed to be the logical extension of a rehabilitation program that really intended to prepare women to return to society as self-reliant and self-supporting members.

The idea to equip each woman's room with a semi-private toilet that provided a level of privacy unknown in men's prisons came from Colorado.

Not only did this indicate a level of decency and humane treatment on the part of the planners, but it also re-enforced the belief that at Shakopee women were expected to behave responsibly.

The groundbreaking ceremony for the new institution was a gala event. It was held on September 19,1984, with Governor Rudy Perpich, Commissioner Orville Pung, Senator Don Samuelson, Representative Mary Forsythe, Mayor Eldon Reinke, Superintendent Jackie Fleming, former Superintendent Ruby Benson, and Jim Zellmer participating. Millie Beneke wrote and directed a play that the women performed. The play featured the ghost of Isabel Higbee repeatedly asking for a new institution, dying once again when her wish was granted, and going on to haunt the institution. Refreshments were served and enjoyed by visitors, staff, and inmates.

The Department of Corrections' biennial reports indicated the need for the new institution. The 1981-82 report stated, "There has been unanimous agreement for years that the Shakopee institution has deteriorated to the point where it is beyond repair and is in need of replacement." Shakopee's average daily population was 60 women and its capacity was 60. The 1983-84 report showed that the average daily population was 69 women. The 1985-86 report showed that the average daily population had risen to 90. Fortunately, in August 1986 the construction of the new institution was completed, and the staff and the inmates moved "across the street." The capacity of the new Shakopee was 132 with five living units: Isabel Higbee which included segregation, Susan B. Anthony, Eleanor Roosevelt, Harriet Tubman, and the Independent Living Center (ILC).

The department's 1987-1988 Biennial Report stated, "Probably the most notable achievement during the biennium was the opening of the state's newest facility for women offenders at Shakopee in August, 1986. Opening of this contemporary institution represents significant progress in eliminating the inequities in what has been provided for women offenders and also makes great advances in addressing the unique needs of women inmates."

The new Shakopee was attractive in many ways, from its warm brick exterior and gabled roofs, to its carpeted hallways that helped to make it a quiet place, to the windows and skylights that brought in the sunlight. The education area had two classrooms on either side of a brightly lit library. The industry area had a custom-made data entry room with plenty of workstations, and each industry supervisor had a separate office. There was a warehouse for the industry program and another for the institution. Food service had gleaming stainless steel work surfaces, lots of space, and plenty of dry, cool, and cold storage spaces.

The living units were well thought out with three levels of privacy for the women: a common area including a small kitchen that was available to all women assigned to that unit, a wing lounge with a phone that was intended only for the women who lived on that wing, and finally, the woman's room that was private for her alone. The women's rooms were also quite attractive with built-in wood wardrobes and wood-framed beds with trundle beds built-in for children. Once again Shakopee would attract visitors from around the world.

Prior to the move "across the street," Barb Hanson arranged to get a huge supply of boxes for free from the glass company in Shakopee. The boxes were actually beer cases that had been misprinted and could not be used as originally intended, but they made sturdy packing containers for the staff and inmates. Each inmate was given 12 boxes for her personal belongings, and on moving day, August 11, 1986, they literally picked up their stuff and walked across the street.

All of the old furniture was left behind, with the exception of a few pieces of furniture that were considered antiques or sentimental favorites by some staff members. Most of those pieces of furniture were placed in the new industry warehouse where they were stored until expedience overruled sentiment, and the old furniture was disposed of.

The women moved their own belongings and the other stuff of the institution across the street to the new buildings. Jackie Fleming recalled how the women were allowed to pick their own rooms. The more senior inmates were allowed to pick first. One woman was allowed to pick again after she discovered that the view from her new window was of the cemetery across the street.

Not only did they pick their own rooms, but they also cleaned their new rooms prior to moving day. Moving the inmates and their belongings only took about two hours, but it wasn't by accident that things worked well.

Jackie Fleming gave credit in her next quarterly report: "Gayle Madigan, the planner, and Carol Buesgens, the actual move supervisor, deserve the accolades for the move without any major problems." When the task of moving was complete, the whole institution celebrated by going swimming at the nearby municipal swimming pool.

In the movie *Field of Dreams*, an Iowa farmer is told, "If you build it, they will come." It seemed that the same thing was true for Shakopee. In 1987-88, the average daily population rose to 124, and by double bunking the women in the ILC, Shakopee's capacity rose to 144. In 1989-90, the average daily population rose to 164. Wing lounges had to be used as dorm rooms. Fortunately in 1991-92, the population fell and the average daily population dropped to 131. Nevertheless, the trend was clear, Shakopee could expect many more women in the future.

The rising population had certain benefits. One benefit was that the institution was able to hire additional staff, including correctional officers, caseworkers, teachers, and industry supervisors. They contributed additional talents and diversity to the institution. Programs were expanded to meet the needs of the increased numbers of women. Greater variety in programming became more feasible.

In the fall of 1986, Roger Knudson became the Education Coordinator for the department at Central Office. Before he left Shakopee, he hired Diane Martinka as a full time ABE/GED instructor and Jeanette June as a half-time Office Technology vocational instructor. Both women were experienced teachers and proved to be excellent instructors and role models for the women at Shakopee.

Diane Martinka recalled that on her first day she was greeted by Ann, the inmate librarian, who said, "Would you like a cup of coffee, Diane?" Ann was very courteous and welcoming. She was also somewhat eccentric, a poet, and a lover of hats. They became good friends. Diane recalled needing to learn the vocabulary of the institution; words like rover, count, kite, and movement had their own special meanings in prison. A kite, for instance, is a written message from an inmate, and staff members were expected to respond in a reasonable length of time.

Having raised a large family prior to teaching at Shakopee, Diane Martinka brought to her work maternal virtues that were a blessing to many of the women: serenity and kindness, a genuine concern for each individual, the ability to find the good in people, and the willingness to do the hard work that needed to be done.

Moving the education area from the basement of Higbee Hall to the new education area was a wonderful improvement. Recalling the new area, Diane said, "It was heaven on earth." Moving the library, however, was a lot of work. It required about 100 boxes filled with books. Diane's husband Bob volunteered and helped with the heavy lifting.The new environment stimulated new programs. Diane Martinka started a National Issues Forum group and a Great Books discussion group with women who had higher academic skills. People from similar groups in the community were invited to visit Shakopee and join in the discussions. In addition, Diane and Mary Strand put on a special event that they called their "Soiree." They wanted to teach the women how to be gracious, how to send out invitations, and how to RSVP. So they sent invitations to all the students inviting them to the "Soiree" and turned their classroom into a gallery. Staff and inmates contributed art and craft items. Father Jim, the Catholic chaplain, was one of the main contributors of art works. Ann, the inmate librarian, read her original poetry, and Sophie, an inmate with a gypsy background, sang songs. Diane and Mary served cookies and lemonade. It was a wonderful soiree.

Diane became the staff advisor for the *Reflector* and the supervisor of the inmate library. She hired inmate librarians and took them shopping for new books at Bookmen, the wholesale bookstore in downtown Minneapolis. She also facilitated inter-library loans with the Scott County Library and picked up and returned books that the county library supplied to the women at Shakopee.

Pat, one of the inmates who requested many books through the inter-library loan system, wrote Diane a thank you note. It began, "Dear-Person-Who-Carries-Books," and it went on to say how extremely grateful she was to Diane even though she didn't know Diane's name. But she appreciated the wonderful service that Diane did for her so faithfully. Pat concluded her note with these words, " In your name I try to do a small act of kindness to another inmate every day."

In order to replace Roger Knudson, Jackie Fleming chose Tom Daly who had 27 years of experience in the field of education, including 10 years as a teacher and assistant education director at Stillwater Prison. Tom was well acquainted with the programming available to men at Stillwater and immediately realized the disparity of services that existed for women. He believed that the women deserved educational programming that was comparable to what men were receiving at Stillwater. Jackie Fleming agreed.

At that time Stillwater had six vocational programs with nine vocational instructors. Each program had a classroom and a shop area. Stillwater's programs were all certified by 916 AVTI. Men at Stillwater could earn certificates from 916 AVTI and credits that were transferable to other vocational colleges. No provision had been made for women in the new institution to have vocational programs and classroom space comparable to what was available to men.

Fortunately, Jeanette June had taught for Hennepin Technical College and her office technology students continued to receive credit from HTC for their work at Shakopee. Her classroom, although new, was much smaller than she needed, but it was a good beginning.

Eventually, Shakopee developed much more classroom space and three full time vocational programs: Office Technology, Horticulture, and Construction Technology. In addition, Desktop Publishing was taught to women at Shakopee, using two-way interactive TV that connected them to the Desktop Publishing classroom at HTC. Jeanette June supervised the desktop students in one corner of her classroom. In 1996 Jeanette and Ralph Schmidtke, the HTC instructor, received a national award for their successful collaboration. In 1998 Jeanette was also selected as Teacher of the Year for the Correctional Education Association's Region IV, which includes six states and two Canadian provinces.

Shakopee women were also way behind the men at Stillwater in college programming. In the 1980s men at Stillwater were able to earn AA and BA degrees and were doing so regularly. No woman had ever earned a college degree while at Shakopee. Too few courses were provided. Tom Daly calculated that at the current rate of college programming at Shakopee it would take nine years for a woman to earn a two-year AA degree. He persuaded Roger Knudson at Central Office to improve college funding for Shakopee. With more courses women began earning college degrees also.

Project Interaction was one of the important reasons for improvements in educational programming at Shakopee. Project Interaction was a small, non-profit corporation that made Shakopee the focus of its generosity. At the heart of Project Interaction was its three-member board made up of Millie and Arnold Beneke and Dorothy Chellsen-Esslinger. Project Interaction began to help the women at Shakopee in the early 1970s by creating the Boutique, the free clothing shop that it set up in a room at the institution. In the years that followed, it donated thousands of dollars for equipment for the photography and pottery programs, for correspondence courses, for college courses, and for nurse's aide training courses. Through its generosity more than 100 women at Shakopee received Certified Nursing Assistant training and certificates.

Millie Beneke was also a playwright and the director of the Buffalo Creek Players at the Glencoe community theatre. Project Interaction brought many plays to the institution for the women's entertainment. Millie wrote many of the plays and Arnold often had a leading role. In July 1991, Millie Beneke was the guest speaker at Shakopee's education awards ceremony that recognized the women's educational achievements. Jackie Fleming used the occasion to recognize the generous contributions of Project Interaction and presented Millie with a plaque expressing the gratitude of the inmates and the staff.

When Jackie Fleming arrived at Shakopee in the fall of 1970, the industry program was nearly non-existent. A few women were involved in sewing clothes for women at Shakopee, but they were not sewing for other state institutions as had been done in earlier years. In addition Commissioner David Fogel informed Jackie Fleming that he would like to see the sewing program end, and Jackie complied.

Superintendent Bergherr had started to set up a data processing program using keypunch equipment, but he intended it to be a training program rather than an industry program. In line with that, Rose Mears was hired on June 1,1971, to train women in keypunch, and she continued to do so until November 30, 1974.

The industry program was reestablished when Judy Luedloff was hired to take over the key punch/data entry program in December 1974. Judy trained women in the use of the equipment and secured contracts with outside agencies and businesses. B. Dalton was one of the good customers that Judy and her women served for many years. The program equipment and training evolved from keypunch, to key to disc, to key to tape, to keying directly to the customer's mainframe. The program also moved from Higbee's basement to Anthony's basement to the new institution where it has been showcased since 1986.

When Judy Luedloff began working at Shakopee, the average daily population was between 35 and 40 women. As the population rose during the next five years, additional work was needed for the women. Light assembly work and telemarketing were added.

The assembly program got a variety of customers and work that included de-burring parts, soldering, and assembling toner boxes, small boxes used in copy machines. Telemarketing/market research included doing market research surveys for Supervalu and telemarketing for Burlington Northern. By 1984, the inmate population was about 80 women, and the industry program sales totaled more than $20,000 per quarter.

When the industry program moved into the new institution in 1986, Judy had three fellow workers, Gary Brown (assembly), Jane Hauer (telemarketing/market research), and Kim Salden (data entry/delivery). They were soon joined by JoEllen Buzinec (textile manufacturing).

JoEllen's program was started, in part, because women at Shakopee were able to succeed where men had failed. The sewing machines and serging machines that were used to equip the textile program came from MCF-Oak Park Heights, the men's maximum-security prison. The industry program there had attempted to have a sewing program, but their security requirements made it difficult to achieve the necessary production standards. Consequently, Oak Park Heights provided Shakopee with the sewing equipment at a very low price.

The quarterly report for July, August, September 1987 suggested that things were going well in the new institution. There were 108 women in the population, well below the capacity of 132. The industry program reported that 42 per cent of the women were employed there either full time or part-time, and sales were up 21 per cent. The education program had nearly 100 women enrolled in its classes during the quarter. Sixty-three of the women had been enrolled in ABE/GED and the Office Technology vocational program.

The first anniversary of the new institution was celebrated with a "special salad" luncheon put on by "Mama D," the well-known Twin City area restaurateur. The new *Inmate Handbook* was issued containing the rules and regulations that became effective September 1, 1987. The handbook was a reminder that Shakopee was still a prison, but the chaplain's report that 34 per cent of the inmates participated in the "Kairos" weekend retreat suggested that it still had a lot of soul. In her summary of the quarter, Jackie Fleming reflected upon the fact that Shakopee continued to operate without a wall or a fence. She attributed this fact to "a dedicated staff and functional building."

The year 1988 was a banner year in several ways. In March the CAMP (Community Alternative for Mothers in Prison) program began with its first woman from Shakopee. CAMP was a collaborative effort between MCF-Shakopee, Genesis II, and Reentry Metro. Pregnant inmates at Shakopee who met the program criteria when they delivered their babies were able to live at Reentry Metro in St. Paul with their babies and attend parenting classes at Genesis II in Minneapolis. Patt Adair, who had been the originator of the parenting program at Shakopee, had become the director of Genesis II and was very instrumental in establishing the CAMP program.

Shakopee was accredited by ACA (the American Correctional Association). The new institution not only passed the test but also received a compliance score of 100 per cent. Jacie Rabideau was the accreditation manager and was a very persuasive taskmaster. The copy machine was nearly exhausted with the multiple examples of documentation that staff members compiled to verify policies and procedures.

Connie Roehrich, who had been serving as the Program Director, was appointed Assistant Superintendent by Jackie Fleming on August 17, 1988. Ken Kimble was hired under a Bush Foundation grant to direct the development of an interactive two-way TV link between Shakopee and Hennepin Technical College. The fiber optic link was completed by the end of

1988. Meanwhile, Judy Luedloff reported that total industry program sales in the 13 years since 1975 had reached $1 million. Within ten years industry program sales averaged over $600,000 per year.

The industry program staff worked hard to expand their program and provide employment for as many women as possible. In June 1989, they reported that 50 per cent of the inmate population was employed full time or part-time in industry (65 of 130 women). Another milestone was reached in March 1990 when Karen Meyer was hired as the first Industry Director for MCF-Shakopee.

Staff training, or the lack of it, became a growing concern for administrators in the Department of Corrections and for Jackie Fleming at Shakopee in the 1970s. The deadly prison riot at Attica in New York in 1971 sent a shock wave through the nation, and the disturbances and law suits that were increasing in Minnesota's correctional facilities signaled that improvements needed to be made. The courts, which had practiced a "hands off" policy toward prisons until the early 1970s, became increasingly active in defining and enforcing minimum standards of health care, procedural due-process in discipline, equal protection under the law, and other constitutional protections guaranteed under the Bill of Rights and the 14th Amendment. The American Correctional Association (ACA) established an accreditation program for correctional institutions in 1974. This provided guidance and pressure on correctional institutions to improve their performance. Staff training was one of the keys to improvement.

At Shakopee Jerry Knutson was hired in 1977 as the volunteer coordinator on a half-time basis. For several years, Jerry recruited volunteers, trained them and coordinated their activities with the programs that they served: recreation, religious programs, and off-grounds activities. Jackie Fleming usually took part in providing some of the training, as did Ricky Littlefield and other staff members.

On the other hand, although new correctional officers were receiving several weeks of training at Central Office, staff training for new staff members at Shakopee was pretty much a hit and miss affair handled by the supervisors of new staff members. When Jackie recognized that new volunteers were getting more comprehensive training than some new staff members, she put Jerry Knutson in charge of staff training also.

Jerry became part of the Training Advisory Committee made up of training directors from the various institutions. They were in communication with and supported by Gerry Anderson, the training director at Central Office. Eventually, certain subject areas became mandatory for all staff, and all full time DOC staff members were required to do 40 hours of training each year. Some of the mandatory areas of training included "Right to Know," "First Aid," and "CPR." The value of taking CPR training became very real when, shortly after taking CPR at Shakopee, Patt Adair saved two young boys at a swimming pool in St. Paul by administering CPR to them.

As the staff training curriculum became more well developed, the staff at Shakopee were able to learn a wide range of subjects from report writing to the latest information on infectious diseases. In addition staff training sessions gave staff members from different parts of the institution the opportunity to become acquainted with each other and learn about each other's duties and concerns. Correctional officers, caseworkers, teachers, industry supervisors, maintenance men, business managers, and administrators became more understanding of each other as they shared staff training experiences.

As the staff training budget grew, it was also used to assist staff members to attend professional conferences such as the National Workshop on Female Offenders as well as conferences sponsored by Blacks in Criminal Justice, Minnesota Correctional Association, and the Correctional Education Association. These conferences helped Shakopee staff members grow professionally, and a number of them made significant contributions on regional and national levels.

Day long training sessions helped to build staff esteem and morale. Getting to know each other, interacting with each other, and brainstorming together were good for the individuals and the staff as a whole. In an interview Jerry Knutson pointed out how staff training days were important "to express to the staff that they are of value" to the institution.

Fiscal year 1989-1990 was a watershed year for Shakopee. Population growth stimulated program development, but resources such as space and funds were not unlimited. The need to purchase bunk beds and to turn wing lounges into bedrooms were early warning signs of future challenges, but for many areas of the institution, things were going pretty well.

Shelby Richardson was hired as the Program Director in February 1989. Shelby had been managing a residential treatment program in Connecticut. She was well acquainted with rehabilitative programs and felt comfortable with Shakopee's program rich environment. When she arrived at Shakopee, the inmate population was under 120, but the population kept increasing. "We kept developing programs," Shelby recalled. "Then we reached critical mass, and we ran out of space."

During the summer of 1989, the new institution reached its capacity of 132 inmates and then went beyond it. The Independent Living Center (ILC), which had apartments and was designed to hold 12 women, was double-bunked to hold 24, and beds were set up in the wing lounges of the other living units.

Industry sales were up over $53,000 in the first quarter. Jeanette June and her vocational program went from half time to full-time. The first greenhouse was completed, and a horticulture vocational program was being planned. For the first time, three college courses were being offered during the same quarter. Five women who completed Nursing Assistant Training were living in the ILC and working off grounds as nursing assistants. The *Reflector* won second prize in the Penal Press competitions.

Not all of the news was so positive. Children's weekend visits were suspended because of security concerns about contraband found in the parenting unit.

On the personnel side, Connie Roehrich, the Assistant Superintendent of Operations, was named Superintendent of MCF-Willow River/Moose Lake. Connie was the first woman to head a male facility, and the first of three women to become wardens or superintendents of other facilities after serving as assistant superintendent at Shakopee. Patt Adair returned to Shakopee and replaced Connie as Assistant Superintendent of Operations.

The rising inmate population was both a blessing and a curse. Education and industry programs ran better with a larger number of women, but higher populations made inmates' lives in the living units more difficult and created more stressful working conditions for correctional officers. Some of the humane aspects of Shakopee like privacy for inmates, children's overnight visiting, off grounds recreation, and correctional officers being allowed to work in civilian clothes were destined to change.

During the last quarter of fiscal year 1989-1990, the average daily population reached 166, which was 22 inmates over the new capacity of 144. Planning began on three new buildings, including two living units that would each house 45 inmates. A new industry building would greatly expand the industry program area, add warehouse space, office space for the business office, and a staff training classroom and offices. Changes were planned for the Higbee living unit, and a ten-bed mental health unit was also planned as an annex to Higbee. Barb Hanson was assigned to be the liaison between Jackie Fleming and the architects and contractors.

On July 2, 1990, Brian Schlottman began the Horticulture vocational class. It was provided under a contract with Hennepin Technical College. The students received credits from HTC and were able to earn diplomas. Before long, attractive gardens were planted at the entrances of nearly every building and in each courtyard. Women planted vegetable gardens as part of the program, and once again women were eating fresh vegetables that they had raised themselves. The horticulture program was therapeutic for inmates, staff, and visitors.

Brian proved to be an excellent instructor and was eventually hired as a state employee. Not only did HTC continue to enroll the women, provide credits and diplomas, but also HTC administrators continued to provide assistance and very beneficial support.

July 1990 was also a good month for the parenting program. Children's visitation on weekends was reinstated. The three-month suspension of the children's overnight visits sent an appropriate message to the women: overnight visits were a privilege that the women must protect with responsible behavior.

The old buildings, now vacant, continued to stand on the six acres of land across the street. As time went on, they fell victim to the local vandals. Discussions were held with Scott County officials about having the county take over the property, but no agreement was reached. Eventually, the officials decided that the institution would retain the property, and by the end of

September 1990, all the old buildings were demolished except a newer maintenance garage that continued to be used for equipment and storage.

In the quarterly report for July-September 1990, Jackie Fleming wrote: "I am pleased with all areas of the institution. Staff are interested, concerned and working hard to improve all of the services we provide. I don't mean that we are perfect as that will never occur, but I do think we are reaching a new level of efficiency and productivity. Thanks to all staff for their continued enthusiasm and hard work."

Overcrowding continued to be a serious challenge. In the fall of 1990, some relief was achieved by transferring 27 women from Shakopee to MCF-Willow River/Moose Lake where a living unit at Moose Lake was made available for them. By the end of March 1991, seventy-one women had been transferred to Moose Lake. One of the benefits for the women at Moose Lake was its new superintendent, Connie Roehrich. She was well acquainted with the women's needs and issues. On the other hand, Moose Lake was about 80 miles farther away from the homes and children of women from the metropolitan area, and it lacked the programming that was available at Shakopee. The new living units that were being planned at Shakopee were not expected to be ready before the summer of 1994.

By June of 1991, several more positive milestones were reached. Two women completed their course of study in Desktop Publishing and were awarded diplomas by Hennepin Technical College. Their success showed that interactive two-way television could deliver instruction as Roger Knudson had hoped it could. In addition a woman who had earned her CNA certificate at Shakopee was able to live in ILC, work off grounds as a nursing assistant, and also complete 14 weeks of training as an Emergency Medical Technician. Programs at Shakopee were helping women turn their lives around.

August 1991 arrived; it was the fifth anniversary of the move "across the street." Five years had passed in the new institution. Jackie Fleming and Patt Adair co-authored an "Anniversary Message" in the August issue of the *Reflector*. The following are excerpts from their article:

"The legacy of Isabel Higbee…who died…while fighting for a separate facility for women, lives on for us as we continue to struggle for equal opportunities for women and parity in treatment…"

"Dedicated to the belief that given the opportunity, respect, dignity and tools for change, women can become independent, self-respecting and self-sufficient, we continue to operate one of the most unique correctional facilities in the country."

"We heartily applaud the efforts of all those who continue to work with us and support our efforts to meet the needs of female offenders in Minnesota."

Jackie and Patt concluded their message by thanking staff, volunteers, DOC personnel, community supporters and the inmates. They wished everyone a happy anniversary. The inmates and staff celebrated the event with an anniversary luncheon and program in food service.

August 1991 had another important date in it, Jackie Fleming's 64th birthday. Jackie was now one year away from retirement. For many staff members at Shakopee, she was the only superintendent they had ever known. She had set the tone; she had been their mentor. She taught them that the inmates were to be called women not girls. From Jackie many had learned to say please and thank you to inmates and to each other. Jackie taught some staff to write clearly and to re-write if necessary. She had often said to her staff, "Remember, you're here for the good of the women." Now she was a year away from retirement, and many people wondered what Shakopee would be like without Jackie Fleming.

Jackie's last year started off very well. Shakopee was once again audited by the ACA, and once again received a score of 100 per cent. Shelby Richardson was the ACA audit manager for Shakopee. The education, industry and program units were cited in the audit for "their diversity and commitment to skill building."

Jackie Fleming had been previously honored as a distinguished alumnus of St. Olaf College and Corrections Person of the Year by the Minnesota Correctional Association. On November 6, 1991, Jackie was honored by AMICUS with the Founders Award.

During the next months, the institution ran well. The inmate population stayed between 132 and 146. Industry sales were up as high as $89,000 in the 4th quarter, and employment ranged between 43 and 53 during the year. Education added Critical Thinking Skills to its ABE/GED program, as well as a math class to its interactive two-way TV classes. The Minnesota State

Services for the Blind taught a course in braille transcription to six long-term inmates. Donna completed the course and began transcribing books into braille. She continued transcribing books for ten years at Shakopee.

Jackie was involved in planning the new buildings and developing the biennial budget, but she knew she would not be at Shakopee when they came into existence. It was a time of change and transition. She addressed these issues in her quarterly report ending fiscal year1991-1992:

"Of immediate concern is planning for future staffing and budget for the next biennium. The completion of the new buildings should occur in the latter part of the biennium so the staffing budget will again have to be divided into now and later. It is becoming increasingly difficult to make any of these decisions as a "lame duck" Superintendent.

"I can't finish 22 years of my life without a few personal comments. I will long remember all of the people I have worked with as we have focused on the woman offender and how to improve her "lot" in life. I would hope that all of you will consistently work for these women who need our help in all areas.

"I have been blessed in working with such excellent staff. It has been because of all of you that we have received national recognition for our programming and humaneness. We have always been a "caring" institution and this has been what has made the difference. I hope this can continue in the future even though the numbers will greatly increase.

" Thank you all for your help and your diligence. It has been sincerely appreciated. I can only wish all of you the best of good luck and a happy future.

"My warmest regards to you all! Jackie."

The July-August 1992 issue of the *Reflector* featured two front-page pictures of Jackie Fleming, one from 1970, the other from 1992. The paper announced that August 21, 1992, would be her 65th birthday and her last day as superintendent. Alma, the inmate editor, promised that a special edition of the *Reflector* was being prepared. She gave some preview quotes from the special edition and also wrote a lengthy article that included a letter from her to Jackie Fleming. In it she told Jackie how grateful she was for what Jackie had given her: “the will to better myself, to think ahead, to make every accomplishment only the beginning of another step forward, and to encourage others to make the most of their opportunities.”

The special edition was very impressive. Twenty inmates and staff contributed articles of appreciation and memories of Jackie Fleming. Connie Hammer, the Senior R.N., remembered how in the old institution Jackie would not get an air conditioner for her office because the inmates didn’t have air conditioning; if they had to tolerate the heat, she would also. Inmates thanked her for being fair, for treating them with respect, for caring about them, for treating them as individuals, and for treating them as women and mothers of children.

Perhaps, Alma, the inmate editor, interpreted best the feelings of inmates and staff when she wrote, “You may be sure, Ms. Fleming, that your name has been written too deeply in their hearts to ever be erased by the passing years.” On Friday, August 21, 1992, the Fleming years came to an end.

On Monday, August 24, 1992, Connie Roehrich became Shakopee's eighth superintendent. It was Connie's 40th birthday. She had 18 years of experience in corrections and criminal justice beginning as a corrections agent at the State Training School in Red Wing in 1974. Connie moved from Red Wing to become a county probation/parole officer in Mankato, and then a senior corrections agent in Glencoe. In 1982 Connie became the unit director for Shaw Cottage at Shakopee. After 18 months Connie left Shakopee and became a federal probation officer. She returned to Shakopee in 1986 when she replaced Patt Adair as Program Director. In 1988 Jackie Fleming appointed Connie to the position of Assistant Superintendent. In 1989, Connie Roehrich became the Superintendent at MCF-Willow River/Moose Lake where she served until Jackie Fleming retired.

Connie Roehrich received a bachelor's degree in social work from Bemidji State University in 1974 and a master's degree in corrections from Mankato State University in 1983. Connie taught a course entitled "Women Offenders" at Metropolitan State University between 1990 and 1995.

Connie Roehrich was the first to admit that she had huge shoes to fill, but she had inherited an institution that was running well. Connie was very well acquainted with Jackie Fleming's philosophy. Jackie Fleming had been a mentor and a role model for Connie. Years later in an interview, Connie recalled how Jackie had taught her about women's mental health issues, and Connie said that in her memory she could still hear things that Jackie said.

Connie Roehrich inherited a number of very capable staff members; one was Barb Hanson. Jackie Fleming appointed Barb acting Assistant Superintendent of Administration in July 1992. Barb was very involved in the planning of the new living units and the new industry building. She was Jackie's liaison with the architects and contractors. Barb provided Connie with a good understanding of the issues related to the new buildings and also the construction projects that were being handled internally by the institution's excellent maintenance staff.

Unfortunately, Connie Roehrich lost Patt Adair who was appointed Superintendent at MCF-Willow River/Moose Lake. Some staff members had been hoping that Patt would become Shakopee's superintendent, and with her departure, they felt they had suffered a double loss, Jackie Fleming and Patt Adair.

The first quarter of fiscal year 1992-1993 ended on September 30, 1992. In her quarterly report Connie Roehrich stated that the budget for FY 94-95 had been completed. It included the new buildings that would add 100 beds including 10 mental health beds. The inmate population was 135. The various programs were running well. Connie also reflected upon the fact that the staff had never had a new Superintendent. While that was true, it was also true that an increasing number of staff had worked in other correctional institutions: Faribault, Lino Lakes, Red Wing, St. Cloud and Stillwater. They brought to Shakopee an increasingly diverse view of how things had been done in the past and how things could be done in the future.

During the remainder of the fiscal year, Connie Roehrich began to assert herself as the superintendent. She asked the staff to "Plan from the Future," to imagine Shakopee in 1995 after the new living units and new industry building had been built and to think about what Shakopee would be like. She asked them to consider what would need to be done to get there.

Each day that followed, the staff and inmates could see the new outer ring of buildings being slowly added to their world. Fortunately, the inmate population also rose slowly.

Meanwhile, more and more women were achieving things for themselves. In June 1993, seven women attended the graduation ceremony at Hennepin Technical College. They proudly wore their caps and gowns as they accepted the diplomas they earned in Horticulture and Electronic Publishing at Shakopee. In the same month, the first woman in Shakopee's history earned her BA degree. She received her degree in cap and gown from Metropolitan State University.

In the fall of 1993, Lt. Nan Herman became the first Captain at MCF-Shakopee. Nan had started working at Shakopee as a correctional counselor in 1979 and became a shift supervisor (CC3) in 1985. In 1986 Nan Herman became the unit director of the Independent Living Center (ILC). Her promotion to Captain seemed to signal that Shakopee and the women had now come of age. Some might wonder if by coming of age the women at Shakopee would lose some of the benefits that smallness had provided: a caring staff, emphasis on rehabilitation, and a concern for women's issues.

Through the summer and fall of 1993, the new buildings rose, a semi-circle of bricks, cement, and steel on the south side of the institution. Bulldozers, cement mixers, construction trailers, pickup trucks and construction workers added to the noise and excitement. Two of the construction workers were women, and they agreed to be interviewed by Chris, the new editor of the *Reflector*.

Mary was a carpenter who had worked on the "new Shakopee" in 1984-86. Pam was an apprentice carpenter who had recently graduated from Project Blueprint. Both were good examples to the women at Shakopee that it was possible for women to get non-traditional jobs at decent pay if they were willing to get the necessary training and do the work.

The new industry building was completed in May 1994, and the industry programs moved into an area that was triple the size of their previous quarters in the core building. The new building also housed the business offices, a staff training classroom and offices, and a large warehouse and loading dock.

The Office Technology/Desktop Publishing and Horticulture vocational classes were able to move into the room that was vacated by the Data Entry industry program. The large room that was vacated by Assembly and Telemarketing would be occupied by Shakopee's third vocational program, Construction Technology.

During the fall of 1993, the education program received a $40,000 Perkins grant for vocational programming, career planning, assessment testing, support services for non-traditional training, and assistance for women upon release. The education program was gearing up to start a non-traditional vocational program. Project Blueprint, a program of Women Venture, was hired under the grant to begin pre-apprenticeship training at Shakopee in the spring of 1994. In the summer Michele Bevis was hired to teach Construction Technology.

Michele Bevis was a woman with construction trades experience whose desire to teach coincided with Shakopee's need to hire a teacher who could be a role model for women. During the next five years she taught women the basic skills needed in the construction trades. Several times they built one-story high practice houses inside their classroom. They also built practical projects such as wooden lawn furniture, saw horses, wooden tool boxes, storage sheds, a special wood storage shed for the Native American sweat lodge, and a large arbor at the entrance of the horticulture greenhouse. Two women from the class were able to go off grounds and re-roof the garage at the Scott County Historical Society site in Shakopee.

The first new living unit to open was the Margaret Mead mental health unit in July 1994. It was attached to the south side of Higbee, and it could accommodate 10 women. The other two new 45-bed living units were opened in successive months. Mary McLeod Bethune unit was opened in August 1994, and Ignacia Broker unit was opened in September. Having 90 beds added, the institution was able to close Tubman temporarily for repainting and maintenance. It would reopen in December 1994. At that point the total number of permanent beds in the institution was 243.

For the next six months the inmate population remained fairly stable, near 200. On April 26-28, Shakopee was audited by the ACA for the third time and once again received a score of 100 per cent. The industry program reported annual sales for fiscal year 1995 of over $500,000 and was employing over 50 per cent of the inmate population. Education's expansion into the old industry area allowed it to open both of its classrooms in the library area for academic uses: ABE/GED in both rooms each day and college classes and GED testing in the evenings. A correctional officer was also added to the education staff. The officer was attached to the Horticulture program so that students could be supervised in the classroom and in the greenhouse/gardens more adequately. A new greenhouse was also built. The students and teachers in the horticulture and construction classes did most of the construction work.

The industry program continued to expand, and under the supervision of Karen Meyer, a computer assisted design/drafting (CADD) program was initiated whereby inmates transferred architectural drawings and blueprints of state buildings to computer discs. The industry program at MCF-Shakopee received the 1996 Innovations Award from the National Association of State Facilities Administrators for this use of CADD.

On July 10, 1996, at the International Correctional Education Association Conference, Jeanette June and Ralph Schmidtke won the Al Maresh Award for the Desktop Publishing Program, a computer-assisted educational program in a correctional setting. The award was given by Plato, Inc. and honored the memory of Al Maresh, the first Education Coordinator for the Minnesota Department of Corrections. Al was a great supporter of the Correctional Education Association and computer-assisted instruction.

As the inmate population continued to rise, some officials in the Department of Corrections analyzed the factors that accounted for the great difference between the inmate population projections of the 1980s and the actual population increases that had occurred by 1995. As they knew, the prison population increases were not due to a marked increase in criminal activity.

The Department of Corrections *Biennial Report for 1996-1997* announced the sobering news: "Two comparisons compiled during the biennium show that Minnesota's prison sentences in terms of actual time served are among the toughest in the nation." One comparison by the U.S. Department of Justice ranked Minnesota second among 27 states surveyed. The second comparison was completed by the Sentencing Guidelines Commission staff. It ranked Minnesota first among 36 states that responded to a national survey.

The report also stated that since 1989, "Strong sentencing enhancements have increased penalties substantially." The report went on to say, "Sentence lengths for more serious crimes doubled..." In short, more men and women were doing more time in prison in Minnesota.

The report also stated that the inmate population at Shakopee had gone over the institution's capacity of 237 despite adding 100 beds in the previous biennium. The report did not make the connection between the "get tough" actions of lawmakers and the overcrowding that was happening at Shakopee and elsewhere in the system.

On the positive side the DOC report did mention several new programs at Shakopee: cognitive restructuring, victim impact classes, and canine companions. Cognitive restructuring was a program established at Shakopee for inmates who were either new to the institution or who returned to the institution after re-offending. The purpose of the program was to explore errors in thinking patterns with an emphasis on how inmates could address problems that lead to incarceration.

Victim impact classes were developed to teach inmates to understand the impact of their crimes on victims, to accept responsibility for their criminal behavior, to learn how to bond with positive people, and to contribute to their communities in ways that would prevent future victimization. At Shakopee the idea of contributing to the community was not new. Inmates there had been contributing to the community in many ways from the very beginning.

Canine Companions was a program at Shakopee for which Connie Roehrich could take a good deal of credit. In an interview Connie recalled how she and several of her staff members visited a women's prison in Tulsa, Oklahoma, as part of a conference on female offenders. During their visit they noticed that a dog was living at the institution. "That started the idea," Connie said. They began to discuss the possibility of having a dog at Shakopee. After gathering more information, Connie invited Joan Barnes, the Regional Director of Canine Companions for Independence, to visit Shakopee. Joan's program trains dogs to work with persons with disabilities. They talked about whether or not inmates might be allowed to give dogs their first year of training. Joan decided that it could work, and Connie gave it her OK.

The first puppy, Hooper arrived at Shakopee in 1994. Hooper was only eight weeks old, a roly-poly puppy, but he grew fast. Leslie was his inmate trainer. Hooper slept in a kennel in Leslie's room and traveled with her throughout the institution. Hooper wore a yellow cloth vest when he was in training/working. The inmates were told to respect his training routine and to always ask Leslie if they could pet him or play with him. Eventually, Hooper was placed with a 16-year old boy in Rochester. Over the next five years, seven puppies received their first year of training with women at Shakopee.

The summer 1999 issue of *The Courier*, the national newsletter of Canine Companions for Independence, pictured Michael Finocharo with his service dog Lucah. Lucah had been trained by Gloria at Shakopee. Another picture showed Kathleen Reinhardt with her service dog Tackett. Tackett had also been trained by Leslie at Shakopee.

The September 30,1999, issue of the Shakopee *Valley News* announced that the Canine Companions for Independence program at Shakopee won the President's Award at the Minnesota Corrections Conference in St. Cloud. Unfortunately, the program ended a short time later.

The art program was another program that flourished during Connie Roehrich's tenure. Some credit must go to the climate of opinion that existed in the 1980s and 1990s. The public in Minnesota was very supportive of the arts, and the legislature echoed that support with legislation that encouraged and even mandated that art works be created for new public buildings. Shakopee's new buildings received some of those art works, but more importantly Shakopee's art program attracted a new teacher.

Therese Mervar started teaching art at Shakopee in 1989. She had interned with Bill Murray, the art instructor at Stillwater, and like him, she was very comfortable working with people in prison. She was a skillful teacher, blessed with patience and compassion.

Although the art program at Shakopee was always a part-time program, in the 1990s it benefited from a number of factors. Project Interaction donated materials and funds to it. A connection developed to the Minneapolis College of Art and Design through Richard Shelton, who taught several classes at Shakopee as part of the expanded college program. The Citizens Council funded some art classes, and AMICUS stepped forward in 1997 and in 1998 to sponsor inmate art exhibits at the Minneapolis College of Art and Design.

The 1998 exhibit in particular was a great success and marked the high point for the art program at Shakopee. The exhibit was entitled Insider Art, 2nd Annual AMICUS Prison Art Exhibition. Art works created by 13 of the women were among the 140 art works matted and framed by interns from the Walker Art Center and exhibited in the main galleries at MCAD from July 17 to August 13.

The opening of the exhibit was a grand affair. Actress Jessica Lange and Penny Winton were honorary co-chairs, and they both spoke at the opening ceremony along with Louise Wolfgram, the president of AMICUS. Jenny Lion, Steve Matheson, and Rich Shelton of MCAD made an hour-long video about the inmate art programs and the exhibition. The video included interviews with inmate artists and several of their instructors. Six women from Shakopee were interviewed as well as Therese Mervar. One of the women artists from Shakopee was able to attend the exhibition. She said that she was honored and humbled by the kind attention she received.

Bill Murray, the Stillwater art instructor, commented on the therapeutic aspect of art programs in prison and how they allow inmates to express things, things that they are unable to talk about. Bill said, "They're able to draw them. They're able to paint them. They're able to share visually what they cannot express verbally."

Diane, an inmate at Shakopee, spoke of the art program in this way, "I needed to find a way back to who I was because I was so completely lost when I came in the doors here. It helped me get some control over my life." Regarding the art exhibition, Therese Mervar said, "It should make us stop and think about those of us on the fringes of society. We all have so much to offer."

Rick Hillengass transferred to Shakopee in June 1997 to become the Assistant Superintendent of Operations. He replaced Terry Carlson who had joined the Adult Facilities Division at Central Office. Rick had a reputation as someone who could be a calming influence and resolve conflicts in the least disruptive ways.

Rick Hillengass had over 20 years of experience in corrections beginning with the college program at Stillwater in 1975 when he was with the University of Minnesota's General College. He next served as the Education Director at MCF-Oak Park Heights and then went on to Central Office as the Assistant Education Coordinator with Dr. Avy Olson. Rick continued in that capacity with Roger Knudson. In 1991 Rick left the education arena and became the Assistant to the Warden at Stillwater and later a unit director. In 1996 Rick transferred to Oak Park Heights as Assistant to the Warden and then to Shakopee.

As the population rose from 258 in June 1997 to 290 in June 1998, 40 bunk beds were added to wing lounges in the older living units, and 24 single rooms in both Bethune and Broker were converted to double rooms. By August 1999, Shakopee's total capacity had increased to 353 with 291 permanent beds and 62 temporary beds. Just 13 years earlier in August 1986, Shakopee was a brand new facility with 132 beds and a population of 90 women. The population had increased 222 per cent in 13 years.

Greater numbers of inmates meant more stress and strain on many parts of the system: more meals to prepare in food service, more heads to count and keep track of in the living units, more mail to inspect and sort in the mail room. More was a problem, but there was also the problem of less. Rick Hillengass reflected on this in a recent interview. He noted that with overcrowding the women have less privacy and less solitude, two very important, humane elements that had been built into the old institution and into the new one. In fact, it had been felt that women needed little or no supervision when they were alone in their own rooms. Hillengass pointed out that one of the few places a woman could be alone was segregation, and although a woman had to violate the rules to get there, for some women it was worth the trouble.

Spring helps to inspire feelings of hope, and in the spring 1998 issue of the *Reflector*, Connie Roehrich wrote an article entitled "Celebrate Spring, Celebrate Life!" In the article, Connie reflected upon the two great religious feasts of springtime, Passover and Easter, and how they promise the hope of freedom from slavery and evil. She concluded her article by saying, "If we have hope, if we believe that good can happen, and if we cooperate with the good around us, we will have good things to celebrate. Just as the gardener must believe in the seeds, the soil, and the sunshine, so we must believe that our hope and our efforts will make our lives better. So open your hearts to hope and celebrate spring, celebrate life."

The education award ceremonies that were held each January and July honored the women who had completed programs in the previous six months. While they celebrated what had been achieved, the ceremonies were also used to inspire the women to continue to improve their educations and their lives. Guest speakers were sought who could inspire the women. In January 1998, Sheila Wellstone spoke to the women. A leader in the fight against domestic abuse, she was very warmly received by the women, many of whom had been victims of physical and sexual abuse.

In July 1998, Cindy Blomgren was the guest speaker. Cindy was a former Shakopee inmate, a graduate of the Desktop Publishing program who had completed her incarceration and was living successfully in the community. The women could identify with her struggle and with her success.

In January 1999, Sister Rita Steinhagen was the guest speaker. She had served a six-month sentence in a federal prison for protesting the infamous

School of the Americas. Following her incarceration, Sister Rita added federal prison reform to her list of things to do.

As the summer of 1998 changed to fall, more attention was paid to the coming gubernatorial election. Skip Humphrey, the DFL candidate, and Norm Coleman, the Republican candidate, were joined by Jesse Ventura, the Independence Party candidate. Jesse Ventura won the governorship with 39 per cent of the popular vote.

Following the election, an announcement came from Central Office that "in line with Jesse Ventura's thinking" there would be no DOC funds available for college programming after June 30, 1999. The announcement came before Ventura took office and before most people had the foggiest notion of Jesse's thinking. A number of DOC staff opposed this assault on the education program. They wrote letters of protest and contacted legislators and other public officials.

After Jesse Ventura was inaugurated and formed a coalition government that included several reputable Republicans and DFLers, things started to look more hopeful. Sheryl Ramstad Hvass was appointed Commissioner of Corrections and visited Shakopee on March 11, 1999. She gave the impression that there was hope for the college program. Commissioner Ramstad Hvass discovered that funds produced by inmates' use of telephones generated enough money to pay for the college program. With those dollars she restored the funding, and it appeared that education programs would be spared.

The threat to the college program, however, was only the beginning. Reduction by attrition was waiting in the wings. The legislature and the governor were committed to giving back a sizable surplus, cutting taxes, and holding the line on spending. With a rising inmate population, the cost of running Shakopee and the other institutions was rising also. Initially, the department chose to cut costs through attrition.

The Construction Technology/Building Trades vocational class was the first to go. When Michele Bevis resigned to pursue other interests, she was not replaced. When Tom Daly retired, he was not replaced. Others wondered when their turn would come, or if they were retiring, what effect that would have on their fellow workers. Morale suffered. Some positions were considered more essential and would not be cut by attrition.

Connie Roehrich was, in fact, the next to leave Shakopee. Her transfer was part of a new policy to move wardens every few years. In an interview that appeared in the September/October issue of the *Reflector*, Connie responded to the question of why she was leaving Shakopee. She said, "The main reason I'm leaving is for my own career development. I believe it's important to rotate people so we all get different working opportunities..."

The policy of rotating wardens was intended to ensure consistency and continuity in the various institutions and made the most sense for the men's institutions. A man who was sentenced to prison might begin his sentence in one institution and transfer to two or more institutions during his incarceration. Consequently, if the rules and policies were the same in the men's institutions, there would be less confusion and fewer difficulties for the inmates and for staff. However, with Shakopee being the only women's institution, the benefits of the new policy to Shakopee were less clear.

Warden Lynn Dingle replaced Connie Roehrich on September 15, 1999. Lynn had come up through the ranks, beginning at Stillwater about 20 years earlier, moving on to Oak Park Heights, and then to Willow River/Moose Lake in 1995 when she was appointed warden. When Lynn Dingle arrived at Shakopee, the inmate population was still rising. On September 30, 1999, the inmate population was 303 women.

Epilogue

My original motivation for writing this history of Shakopee was really twofold: to discover more fully who Isabel Higbee was and to record the history of the Fleming years. Most inmates and staff at Shakopee knew very little about Isabel Higbee beyond the facts that were on the plaque dedicating a building to her memory. After Jackie Fleming retired, it seemed that new staff coming to Shakopee deserved to know what Jackie had tried to do and what she had accomplished. Those of us who had benefited from her leadership continued to be guided by her vision, but many of us were destined to leave within a few years and would not be available to provide that background information.

This book began when I did a two-hour taped interview with Jackie Fleming in 1998. It was the first of 20 interviews with women and men who had worked at Shakopee. The information on Isabel Higbee was a little harder to find and included a visit to Carleton College, where some of her correspondence is located. When I discovered that Florence Monahan had written a book, *Women in Crime*, about her first 20 years in corrections, writing about those early years became much easier. I read in Monahan's book that six years after she left Shakopee someone wrote a history of the institution and failed to mention her at all. I decided that I would do my best to mention each superintendent in this history.

Focusing on the superintendents and the highlights of their years seemed to be a reasonable approach to telling the story of the institution, but it has its shortcomings. The humanity of the inmates and their stories are mostly untold, as are the stories of the staff women and men in the trenches: the correctional counselors/officers, the maintenance men, the nurses, the clerical staff, the teachers, the industry supervisors, and the many volunteers.

I hope that what I have written is factual and provides enough of a skeleton that future writers will have an easier time telling the story of the institution and the women for whom it was built.

I toured Shakopee on September 26, 2003, and I learned that the inmate population was 419. Three areas were under construction: the visiting room and food service were being expanded, and the ILC was being converted from six apartments for 24 women into a 24 room living unit for 48 women.

Warden Lynn Dingle had left Shakopee after two years to become the warden at Oak Park Heights. Rick Hillengass served as acting warden from September 26, 2001, until February 3, 2003, when Mark Carey became the new warden.

Budget constraints continued to affect the institution. When Industry's Judy Luedloff retired, no one was hired to replace her; the burden of her work was shifted among the remaining staff. The CADD program and Occupational Therapy were eliminated. The Art program, Horticulture and Desktop Publishing vocational programs, and the college program were all eliminated by July1, 2003. Caseworkers were carrying heavier caseloads. Correctional officers and maintenance men were "doing more with less." That day I saw many good people working to help the women make things better for themselves. In the classrooms, industry shops, and living units, women were studying, tutoring, working, and doing CD treatment.

The new living unit that is named after Florence Monahan is the treatment unit. That seems very appropriate because each woman holds the key to her own rehabilitation. As Florence Monahan said, "Unless a woman herself wishes to change, no improvement can be made in her character."

My thanks to the many women and men who have helped me tell this story and who believe that their work at Shakopee was "for the good of the women."

Thomas M. Daly
September 29, 2003

Poetry

Our Paper

Now we're starting a newspaper
"The Reflector" is its name.
We're printing it just for us girls
But striving too for fame.

That it will be successful
Is surely our desire,
And when it comes to reading it,
May no one ever tire.

Margaret A.'s elected editor,
Now we know she's mighty proud;
We hope she'll have the best
of luck
With best wishes from the crowd.

Then, too, we hope in a year or so,
That we can contemplate
The sending of this paper
To four corners of the state.

Don't ever think this paper
Is going to be dead
As we'll fill it full of humor
'Til your very face is red.

Good luck to the "Reflector"
We hope it ceases never,
But will until the end of time
Go on and on forever.

Marie Carey

Our School

Miss Toner wants some poetry,
So I will try my best
To satisfy her little want,
Though it will be a jest.

The classes start at eight o'clock,
And do not end till five;
And though Miss Toner never tires,
I'm s'prised that she's alive.

One day we have arithmetic,
The next day is for maps;
And lo! The next day English puts
Red hot into our laps.

Our library, it is the "tops,"
The very latest books,
And magazines right off the press,
Fill up our reading nooks.

We have exhibits good to see
Of paper, wood, and stone,
And then one of aluminum,
That are our very own.

We know our school cannot be beat,
Of that we all are sure,
For "fevers" to attend their classes
The girls say there's no cure.

For our "Reflector" just a word,
The pride of girls and staff.

It takes in our "Society,"
And now and then a laugh.

We strive each month to make it grow,
And make improvements, too.
We hope Miss Jamieson is pleased,
And all our readers, too.

Marie Carey

Untitled

Between the dark and the daylight
When dawn is beginning to break,
The roosters start crowing,
Each other out-doing,
And oh, what a noise they make.

They seem to have duets and trios,
And quartettes, and also a choir.
Oh, for a rooster to put
in the roaster,
Then throw some more coal
on the fire.

You can hear them from
Shaw and Higbee,
From Sanford and Anthony, too.
I'd sure like a plump one
To serve with a dumplin',
Or roast it with dressing, or stew.

It only would be the Death angel
Could quiet a rooster or two.
Thanksgiving is nearing
For which we are cheering.
Hope Weiner is fattened.
Don't you?

Jessie Geitz

Dad

His hair has turned a little gray,
His shoulders stoop a bit,
But his eyes retain their sparkle,
And he has the same old grit.

When I was just a little tyke,
I'd climb upon his knee,
And listen to his boyhood yarns;
How they inspired me!

His kindness and his patience are
The things I can't forget;
The few spanks that he gave to me
I surely won't forget.

He's been my pal in many things;
I'm happy that I've had
Him standing at my side.
That man, whom I call dad.

Marie Carey

Remembering

When you sit alone at the
end of the
day
It's funny the thoughts that come
wending your way
You wonder how ever you
did this and
that
And how in the world
you got where
you're at.
Money, success, and friends
that were
true
All of these once belonged to
you. They tell you, "Forget and start
anew." But that's not so very easy to do.
Thoughts of the past come to your
mind. If one could forget, it would be
so kind,
When you sit alone and
the tears start
to fall'
The thought of what might
have been
hurts most of all.

Philomine Shepard

When Lilacs Bloom

When Lilacs bloom in the
month of May,
We know that summer's
on the way,
They fill the air with
sweet perfume,
And adorn their bushes with beauteous
bloom

It seems romance is in the air,
And youth makes much
of lady fair.
Then lady's freedom meets
its doom,
There are wedding bells when lilacs
bloom.

A toddling youngster loves to play,
In her great "palace" through
the day
Amid the bushes she
makes a room;
And sings to her dolly, when
lilacs bloom.

Then life seems good to everyone
We're glad that winter's
over, done.
Long may the lilacs wave
their plumes,
It's happy time when the
lilac blooms.

Blanche Greenlee

In Jail (with apologies to R. L.S.)

In winter we get up at night
And dress by our electric light
In summer quite the other way
We have to go to bed by day.

Well, I don't like this prison life,
'cause doing time is only strife;
We get into our neighbor's hair
And on her nerves we're
wear and tear.

We're "excused" here and "excused"
there;
We're not supposed to have
one care,
But "Time" will get us in the end;
That's if our ways we do
not mend.

Now, ladies, let me put you wise:
On "Old John Law" there
are no flies;
We cannot beat him,
though we're smart;
The penalty is surely tart.

Let's stay outside where
we will rate
A better bedtime than at eight
When we get up 'twill be daylight
When we retire it will be night.

Marie Carey

Let Me Remember

Let me remember
Only these things,
Now that we are apart;

Your eyes as you smiled
At my silly whims,
Your smile as you helped
In every way you could;
Your hands so tender and dear,
Your arms about me
Holding me close,
The roughness of your coat
Against my cheek,
Your lips pressed against mine,
Pledging your love.

Only these, my dear,
Let me remember.

Lucille Cooke

My Mother

She carried me under her heart,
Loved me before I was born,
Put her hand in God's and
walked through
The valley of shadows that I
might live.

Bathed me when I was helpless,
Rocked me when I was weary,
Nestled me on pillows softer than

down,
And sang to me in the voice of an
angel.

Held my hand when I learned to walk,
Nursed me when I was sick,
And while I knelt at her side,
Taught my lips to pray.

Through all the days of my youth
She gave me strength for my weakness
Courage for my despair, and hope
To fill my hopeless heart.

She was loyal when others failed
Was true when tried by fire,
Loved me when I was unlovely,
Was my friend when other
friends were gone.

I wish I could tell her today,
How I wanted to be the person
She wanted me to be,
And all the other things I left
unsaid ---too long.

Lucille Cooke

Untitled

The birds are singing in the trees,
The flowers are bright and gay;
I sit and sew on B. V. D.'s
For fifteen cents a day.

Jessie Geitz

Untitled

I often wish I had a twin,
Then I'd go out and she'd come in.

Catherine West

Photo Album

Photo courtesy of the Minnesota Historical Society

The original Stillwater State Prision circa 1910

Photo courtesy of the Minnesota Historical Society

Women inmates in Stillwater Prision circa 1910

Photo courtesy of the Minnesota Historical Society

Isabel Higbee Hall at Shakopee in 1936

Photo courtesy of the Minnesota Historical Society

The plaque dedicating Isabel Higbee Hall in 1920

Photo courtesy of the Minnesota Historical Society

Women at Shakopee with Florence Monahan in center

Photo courtesy of the Minnesota Historical Society

Women working on the farm at Shakopee

Women posing with one of their haystacks

Photo courtesy of the Minnesota Historical Society

Photo courtesy of the Minnesota Historical Society

Women working in the sewing room in Anthony Cottage

Photo courtesy of the Minnesota Historical Society

The State Reformatory for Women at Shakopee in 1937

Photo courtesy of the Minnesota Historical Society

Aerial view of the farm at Shakopee in 1950

Superintendent Florence Monahan 1920-1932

Photos courtesy of MCF-Shakopee

Superintendent Jackie Fleming 1970-1992

The new MCF-Shakopee

Photo by T.M. Daly

Florence Monahan Living Unit

Photo by T.M. Daly

Photo by T.M. Daly

Entrance to MCF-Shakopee

Bibliography

Monahan, Florence. *Women in Crime*. New York: Ives Washburn, 1944.

Morris, Norval; and Rothman, David J.,ed. *The Oxford History of the Prison*. New York: Oxford University Press, 1995.

Pittman, Rose Marie, ed. *WSR (Women's State Reformatory) Anthology of Verse*. Shakopee: The Academic Department, 1940.

Women's State Reformatory: Biennial Reports 1921 – 1936. Shakopee, 1936.

Winter, Alice Ames. "Shakopee," *Ladies Home Journal*. December, 1925.

Interviews

Patt Adair, Warden, MCF-St.Cloud

Bob Bergherr, Superintendent, MCF-Shakopee

JoEllen Buzinec, Textile Manufacturing Supervisor

Jackie Fleming, Superintendent, MCF-Shakopee

Barb Hanson, Associate Warden of Administration

Nan Herman, Captain

Rick Hillengass, Associate Warden of Operations

Roger Knudson, Teacher/Education Director

Jerry Knutson, Employee Development Director

Mickey Kopfmann, Residential Program Manager

Barb Landoe, Chemical Dependency Treatment Coordinator

Rickey Littlefield, Volunteer Coordinator

Judy Luedloff, Data Processing Supervisor

Diane Martinka, ABE/GED Instructor

Irene Powers, Correctional Counselor

Shelby Richardson, Program Director

Connie Roehrich, Warden, MCF-Fairbault

Jim Salmon, Director, Anthony Living Unit

Shirley Shumate, Chemical Dependency Treatment Coordinator

Jim Zellmer, Director of Institutional Support Services

*Note to reader: titles listed refer to the positions held while associated with MCF-Shakopee with the exceptions of Patt Adair and Connie Roehrich who are currently wardens at their respective institutions

Newspapers

MCF-Shakopee *Reflector*

Minneapolis *Journal*

Minneapolis *Star*

Minneapolis *Tribune*

Minnesota *Women's Press*

St. Paul *Dispatch*

St. Paul *Pioneer Press*

Shakopee *Valley News*